A L I E N

AUGMENTED REALITY SURVIVAL MANUAL

THIS IS A CARLTON BOOK
Published by Carlton Books Limited
20 Mortimer Street
London W1T 3JW

A CIP catalogue for this book is available from the British Library.

ISBN 978-1-78739-004-1

Printed in China

10 9 8 7 6 5 4 3 2 1

Editorial Director: Roland Hall
Design: Russell Knowles
Production: Emily Noto

U.S.C.M.

THE UNITED STATES COLONIAL MARINE CORPS

ALEN

AUGMENTED REALITY SURVIVAL MANUAL

OWEN WILLIAMS

g

GOODMAN

CONTENTS

CASE STUDY

2089CE
USCSS PROMETHEUS

CASE STUDY

2104CE
USCSS COVENANT

Fig. A.

A NEOMORPH SKETCH BY
THE SYNTHETIC 'DAVID'
WHILE ON BOARD *USCSS*
PROMETHEUS, 2089CE.

PROPERTY OF U.S.C.M.

ALIEN SURVIVAL MANUAL
WITH AUGMENTED REALITY

CONTINUE YOUR BASIC TRAINING BEYOND THE
PAGES OF THIS HYBRID BOOK.

WARNING!
CONTAINS
AUGMENTED
REALITY

1

DOWNLOAD THE FREE
ALIEN AR APP
from www.apple.com/itunes or
www.android.com/apps and open it on your
smart device.

Download on the App Store

GET IT ON Google Play

2

AR VIDEO

SCAN THE PAGES WITH THESE
INTERACTIVE ICONS...

AUGMENTED REALITY

3

#1
XENOMORPH EGG
SIMULATION

PRIMARY OBJECTIVE:

SECONDARY OBJECTIVE:

AR
VIDEO

AR-fueled images
activate videos from
five *Alien* movies to
your smart device.

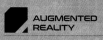
AUGMENTED
REALITY

Access seven fully
interactive training
exercises on your
smartphone or tablet.

SEVEN
FULLY INTERACTIVE
AR EXPERIENCES

Eggs possess a rudimentary nervous system, linked to a network of veins. These allow the Egg to perceive when a possible host is detected nearby.

It is capable of shooting a stream of flame up to 30 meters. This range can be extended by firing the flame upwards, causing the stream to arc down onto a target.

Powered by **Digital Magic**®

U.S.C.M.
THE UNITED STATES COLONIAL MARINE CORPS

" IF IT MOVES, KILL IT.
IF IT DOESN'T MOVE—
KILL IT AGAIN. "

—MARINE CORP. MAXIM

FIGHT OR DIE:
U.S.C.M. FOUNDATION

MARINE, WELCOME TO UNITED STATES COLONIAL MARINE CORP. YOUR BASIC TRAINING HAS BEGUN.
MAKE NO MISTAKE: YOU ARE GOING TO WAR.

The circumstances of that conflict, however, will be different to anything you may have seen, heard, or read about from previous military theaters. The threat posed by the alien creatures known as Xenomorphs is unprecedented. The following pages are therefore designed to prepare you—as far as preparation is possible—for the enemy you now face. Descriptions of the alien's characteristics will be followed by some reminders of tactical procedures and a précis of key U.S.C.M. equipment.

Most important, detailed case studies of previous documented encounters with the Xenomorph follow: both military and civilian. Study these scenarios carefully and memorize them thoroughly. You will learn from the successes of these previous combatants. But perhaps even more crucially, you will learn from their far more frequent failures and defeats. Do not mistake the Xenomorph for a dumb animal. Its ruthless cunning, ferocious strength, and extraordinary speed must never, under any circumstances, be underestimated.

HIGHLY CLASSIFIED: You may have come upon intelligence regarding attempts to capture the Xenomorph for study and reconditioning. Some departments within the Weyland-Yutani Corporation, including the Bio-weapons division, have indeed theorized that the Xenomorph's unique power could one day be harnessed and weaponized in the service of humankind. These classified investigations are ongoing, but they are not your concern. Unless explicitly ordered, do not attempt to capture or subdue the Xenomorph. Such endeavors have historically only ended in disaster, with containment proving challenging. Your mission is to exterminate and eradicate the Xenomorph threat wherever it is encountered.

"All right sweethearts, you heard the man and you know the drill. Assholes and elbows!"

PROPERTY OF U.S.C.M.

COLONIAL MARINES
U.S.C.M. HISTORY

The U.S.C.M. accounts for more than 165,000 personnel across four divisions, with just under 60,000 those in active service at any given time. Each division is organized into three units: Assault Units, Ri Platoons, and Squads: "Colonial Marines are very tough hombres. They're packing state-of-the-art fir power, there's nothing they can't handle." Carter J. Burke.

ASSAULT UNITS

Formed of battalions equipped for independent deep-space operations where backup is unavailable, these units encompass reconnaissance, sniper squads, combat engineers, and heavy ordnance, as well as non-combatant medical personnel.

RIFLE PLATOONS

These active aggressive units are small, breakaway infantry units operating from UD-4 drop-ships. A typical eight-man platoon may be assisted by one or two synthetics acting as tech advisors or scientists.

SQUAD

Squads are even smaller sub units, consisting of four Marines forming two fire teams: one armed with M41 pulse rifles and the other carrying an M41 and an M56 Smart Gun.

ANYTIME, ANYWHERE

The United States Colonial Marine Corps (U.S.C.M.C., or U.S.C.M.) is a force kept in perpetual readiness for operations in off-world environments. Officially ratified by the National Security Act of 2101, it superseded the more traditionally terrestrial U.S. Marine Corps.

WE ENDANGER NON-HUMAN SPECIES

The U.S.C.M.C. is now part of the United Americas Allied Command (U.A.A.C.); the U.A. being the single socio economic block comprised of the former North, Central, and South Americas officially merged in 2104. The U.S.C.M.C.'s primary function is to protect the U.A.'s interests in its off-world colonies, although in crises they may also undertake aggressive action.

LEAN & MEAN

The Aerospace wing of the U.S.C.M.C. is divided among Drop Groups, Tactical Groups, and Support Groups. DGs operate with ground troops as backup. TGs undertake reconnaissance, ground attack, and air superiority missions. SGs are concerned with evacuation and search-and-rescue missions.

WEYLAND-YUTANI CORP

CORPORATE OWNERSHIP

The U.S.C.M.C. is owned by the Weyland-Yutani Corporation and has occasionally been co-opted by the company to protect its own interests. The events on LV-426 (Acheron) in 2178 are an example of such an operation: CMs were dispatched aboard the USS *Sulaco* to investigate loss of contact with the colony and neutralize a Xenomorph hive.

WEYLAND-YUTANI CORP

THE COMPANY:
WEYLAND-YUTANI CORP

Often referred to as Wey-Yu or simply "The Company," The Weyland-Yutani Corp is a multinational corporate giant operating both on Earth and beyond. Such is the size of the conglomerate, its stock value is almost incalculable, but is certainly in the many trillions of dollars. It is principally a technology manufacturer and supplier; its products include synthetics, spacecraft, weapons, and computing equipment. However, it also owns and supplies the United States Marine Corps; operates terraforming projects on multiple planets (via the use of its own patented atmosphere processing plants); and oversees correctional facilities. In fact, it is difficult to identify industries in which Weyland-Yutani is not involved. The Company even has interests in brewing and in prison-based auto racing.

Weyland-Yutani was formed in 2099 following a hostile take-over of the Yutani Corporation by Weyland Corp.

Weyland Corp was a British company established by Sir Peter Weyland in 2012, that quickly achieved immense success in the areas of technology, research, and development. The most notable achievements were major advancements in faster-than-light travel and hypersleep; terraforming and off-world colonization; medical technology; and synthetic design beginning with the "David" android line.

The Yutani Corporation was a Japanese cybernetics start-up operating in the early twenty-first Century. A dispute with Weyland Corp over the "David" patent led to its being absorbed into the rival company in 2099.

Since its first encounter with the Engineer species in 2093, Weyland (and subsequently Weyland-Yutani) has been pursuing the immense possibilities in harnessing the Xenomorph as a bio-weapon. Wey-Yu vessels and operatives were intimately involved in the situations on and around LV-426/Acheron in 2122 and 2179; and the correctional unit on Fiorina "Fury" 161, also in 2179. While not directly involved, it was closely monitoring the United System's Military's attempts to reverse bio-engineer the Xenomorph species aboard the USM *Auriga* in 2381.

ARMAT M42A RIFLE

U.S.C.M.
U.S.S. SULACO
COLONIAL MARINES
2nd BATT 9th REGT.

2089CE

USCSS

PROMETHEUS

MISSION DETAILS

In 2089, an expedition led by Dr. Elizabeth Shaw discovered cave paintings in Scotland that appeared to show primitive men in thrall to an alien being, pointing to a particular group of stars.

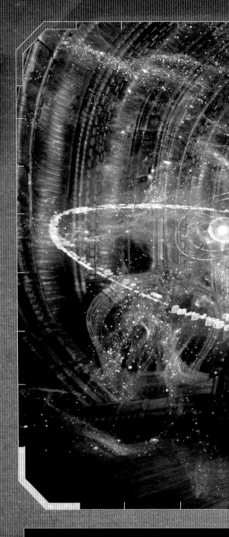

Two years later, under contract to Weyland Corp, the USCSS *Prometheus* began its journey to the indicated Zeta 2 Reticuli star system, and specifically to LV-223—one of the gas giant Calpamos' three moons.

Arriving after a two-year flight, the crew—including Shaw, Captain Janek, archaeologist Charles Holloway, biologists Milburn and Fifield, Weyland employee Meredith Vickers, and a "David" synthetic—discovered a derelict Engineer spacecraft with a sizable cargo of urn like Steatite Ampules. Due to frankly inexplicable lapses in safety protocols, Milburn and Fifield were infected by organisms on the moon's surface, and an ampule was brought back aboard the Prometheus and found to contain the mutagenic pathogen A03959X.91-15, since then colloquially dubbed "black goo."

Misinterpreting prior instructions from Sir Peter Weyland, David made the decision to experiment with the goo on human subjects. He deliberately infected Holloway, who in turn transmitted the "infection" to Shaw, resulting in the gestation of a squidlike "trilobite" creature within her womb. Shaw was able to remove the creature surgically using a MedPod, but she was not able to contain it, resulting in its escape and rapid growth.

Having been awakened from apparent prolonged hibernation, a lone surviving Engineer was responsible for the deaths of several more *Prometheus* crew and the decapitation of David, but he was thwarted in his attempt to launch the derelict ship by Janek's crashing the *Prometheus* into it. Shaw later encountered both the Engineer and the trilobite in the *Prometheus*' lifeboat, but escaped with David's still functioning head in a second derelict.

Uncorroborated reports suggest that the trilobite's attack on the Engineer resulted in the latter's gestation of the creature known as the "Deacon."

ABOVE RIGHT: AN ADVANCED MAPPING SYSTEM THAT FORMED PART OF THE "ENGINEER"'S SHIP NAVIGATION.

RIGHT: THE SCIENTIFIC VESSEL USCSS PROMETHEUS PRIOR TO ITS VOYAGE TO LV-223.

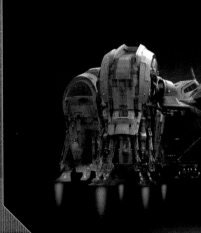

PROMETHEUS

THE EARLIEST RECORDED
ENCOUNTER WITH THE
ALIEN SPECIES KNOWN AS
XENOMORPHS RESULTED IN
THE TERMINATION OF ALMOST
ALL INVOLVED: HUMAN, ALIEN,
AND SYNTHETIC.

BUILDING BETTER WORLDS

WEYLAND MEGACORP

ELIZABETH SHAW

British archaeologist and paleontologist credited with the discovery of the Engineer homeworld LV-223 and instrumental in setting up the 2091 *Prometheus* expedition. The daughter of a missionary, her spiritual upbringing informed her understanding of the Engineers as the creators of humankind; Shaw believed the *Prometheus* mission was a quest to find God.

MEREDITH VICKERS

Acting CEO of Weyland Corp and daughter of founder Peter Weyland. Vickers understood the *Prometheus* mission was a fool's errand, but she agreed to act as its director. Her clandestine secondary mission was to monitor her father, who was secretly aboard.

CHARLES HOLLOWAY

Archaeologist, and Shaw's more skeptical partner. What Holloway lacked in spiritual zeal he made up for in his thirst for knowledge and adventure.

JANEK

Captain of the USCSS *Prometheus*. Largely uninterested in the details of the mission itself, but fiercely dedicated to the safety of his crew.

FIFIELD

Geologist with many years' experience, although he appeared to have developed some form of personality disorder by the time of the *Prometheus* mission.

MILBURN

A biologist whose catastrophic lapse of judgement when confronted with LV-223's mutated indigenous fauna led to his own death and that of Fifield.

DAVID

Weyland Corp's 8-series of "David" androids, with twice the intelligence and several times the strength of the average human. Programmed to display intense curiosity and to doggedly pursue projects to their conclusion. Emotional and ethical protocols were deemed unnecessary by the Company.

PETER WEYLAND

Billionaire entrepreneur, inventor, and founder of Weyland Corp. Awarded the Nobel Prize for curing cancer in 2023. Funded the *Prometheus* mission in 2091 at the age of 101, hoping to discover the secret of immortality. Revealed to be actually aboard the *Prometheus* unbeknown to most of its crew. Did not survive first contact with the "Engineers."

USCSS PROMETHEUS

The USCSS *Prometheus* was constructed specifically for its namesake mission, but its trillion-dollar cost threatened to destroy even the immensely powerful and profitable Weyland Corp. The most advanced starship ever designed and built up to that point, it was powered by four nuclear ion plasma engines, had light-speed capability, and measured a comparatively modest 425 feet long, 160 feet wide, and 120 feet high.

The ship carried 17 hypersleep chambers, allowing for a maximum of 17 crew members (plus synthetics, which can travel interstellar distances without hibernation). Other equipment included an RT Series Group Transport and a much smaller two-man ATV NR6, both for surface travel; eight individual crew escape pods; one much larger seven-room escape pod (or "lifeboat"); and a Pauling MedPod 720i. The latter was nominally calibrated for only male use (and specifically for the use of the centenarian Peter Weyland), but was overridden by Shaw for her emergency self-caesarean section when dealing with the trilobite.

The lifeboat was disguised as Vickers' own personal suite, and it would have been capable of sustaining occupants, in or out of hypersleep, for 50 years, had it not immediately crashed on launch.

RIGHT: PROMETHEUS IN SPACE FLIGHT.
BELOW RIGHT: A FLYPAST FEATURING THE USCSS PROMETHEUS.
BELOW: THE CREW EXPLORE ON THE SURFACE OF LV-223.

PERSONNEL:

+ JANEK
+ CHARLIE HOLLOWAY
+ ELIZABETH SHAW
+ DAVID
+ MEREDITH VICKERS
+ FIFIELD
+ MILLBURN

RESTRICTED CASE FILE:
ENGINEERS AND BLACK GOO

ENGINEERS

Technologically advanced alien life-form of unknown origin, thought to be the progenitors of the human race. As tall as 9 feet, they are muscular, hairless humanoids with albino complexions. Clearly masters of technology, particularly bioengineering, it is thought the Engineers probably "seeded" multiple planets with biological life along with Earth. For reasons unknown, they appeared to have become hostile toward their creations on Earth, although an apparent plan to wipe out humankind with cargo ships of weaponized black goo appeared to have gone catastrophically awry by the time of USCSS *Prometheus'* arrival on LV-223.

PROMETHEUS

"DEACON"

Little is known about the creature—dubbed the "Deacon" due to the shape of its skull—glimpsed on LV-223 in 2094. It seems clear, however, that while undeniably physically similar, the creature was not a Xenomorph. Company scientists hypothesize that it is instead a by-product of the Engineer chemical colloquially known as "black goo," intended for use as a bio weapon. If we assume that the Xenomorph species itself was originally deliberately bio engineered, the Deacon may be an earlier, abandoned iteration. Research is ongoing.

"TRILOBITE"

This squidlike creature appears to be an earlier iteration of the Facehugger, performing a similar function but significantly larger in size. Reports on its gestation are confusing and contradictory, but its ultimate genesis seems to trace back to the reaction of "black goo" with human reproductive material. The only known example was found onboard the USCSS *Prometheus'* within Dr. Elizabeth Shaw, but it was surgically removed before reaching its final form. Its subsequent attachment to, and impregnation, of an Engineer resulted in the "birth" of the Deacon.

"BLACK GOO"

Chemical agent A0-3959X.91-15 is a mutagenic pathogen manufactured by the Engineer species, comprised of micro-organisms that immediately begin to aggressively mutate inside any exposed host. Its witnessed effects on LV-223 in 2093 included the creation of the Trilobite from Holloway's reproductive material; the growth of indigenous worms into snake-like "Hammerpedes"; and the increased strength coupled with severe rage of the infected Fifield.

RIGHT: THE PROMETHEUS CREW ENCOUNTERED VASELIKE OBJECTS ON LV-223.

MARINE BASIC TRAINING:
HOW TO KILL ALIENS

The Xenomorph is a hardy species, capable of survival in multiple environments. Documented encounters with the creature to date have thankfully been limited to relatively unpopulated locations, such as spacecraft, a colony village, and a prison moon. Their adaptability and intelligence, however, makes the thought of an outbreak in a populous area extremely troubling. There are few conditions in which the organism does not thrive.

SPACE

Shipboard encounters with the Xenomorph have been the norm thus far, allowing the organism to use similar tactics to those employed in indoor land-base environments. However, several reports indicate that the alien species is more than capable of subsisting in the vacuum of space itself, surviving in open airlocks and on the outer hulls of space vessels. Data is lacking on whether its survival in such conditions is temporary or indefinite.

WATER

Water-base encounters with the Xenomorph have been rare, but the events aboard the USM Auriga in 2379 proved that the creature demonstrates significant subaquatic capabilities. They are thought not to have lungs—which may also explain their ability to function in vacuum conditions—but Company scientists have hypothesized that the dorsal spines present on some branches of the Xenomorph genus may function as air filters. There was even once a school of thought suggesting the creatures' home planet may be mainly amphibious.

BELOW: THE CATERPILLAR P-5000 POWER LOADER PROVED TO BE A FORMIDABLE TOOL AGAINST AN ALIEN QUEEN.

LAND

Recorded encounters with the alien have largely taken place in enclosed spaces, such as the Hadley's Hope colony on LV-426. These provide the organism with ample opportunities for nesting, stalking, and hiding, and the creatures have displayed a surprising ability to navigate structures via ducting and crawl spaces. Seemingly particularly at home on desolate moons, anecdotal, uncorroborated evidence nevertheless indicates them to be equally effective opponents in tropical and Arctic conditions.

RIGHT: USE ANY HARDWARE AVAILABLE, IN THIS CASE AN M577 APC.

BELOW: AVOID CONFINED SPACES.

USCSS *PROMETHEUS* TRANSMISSIONS

TRANSMISSIONS FROM THE FIELD CAN PROVIDE VALUABLE INFORMATION ABOUT THE HISTORY AND ORIGINS OF THE ALIEN THREAT. THE FOLLOWING WERE ALL RECEIVED AROUND THE USCSS PROMETHEUS INTERACTION IN 2089.

" THIS IS OUR MOST RECENT DISCOVERY. IT'S A 35,000-YEAR-OLD CAVE PAINTING FROM THE ISLE OF SKYE IN SCOTLAND. THESE ARE ANCIENT CIVILIZATIONS, THEY WERE SEPARATED BY CENTURIES, THEY SHARED NO CONTACT WITH ONE ANOTHER, AND YET THE SAME PICTOGRAM, SHOWING MEN WORSHIPPING GIANT BEINGS POINTING TO THE STARS WAS DISCOVERED AT EVERY LAST ONE OF THEM. THE ONLY GALACTIC SYSTEM THAT MATCHED WAS SO FAR FROM EARTH THAT THERE'S NO WAY THAT THESE PRIMITIVE ANCIENT CIVILIZATIONS COULD HAVE POSSIBLY KNOWN ABOUT IT. BUT IT JUST SO HAPPENS, THAT SYSTEM HAS A SUN, A LOT LIKE OURS. AND BASED ON OUR LONG-RANGE SCANS, THERE SEEMED TO BE A PLANET. JUST ONE PLANET WITH A MOON, CAPABLE OF SUSTAINING LIFE. AND WE ARRIVED THERE THIS MORNING. "

—CHARLES HOLLOWAY

" FINAL REPORT OF THE VESSEL *PROMETHEUS*. THE SHIP AND HER ENTIRE CREW ARE GONE. IF YOU'RE RECEIVING THIS TRANSMISSION, MAKE NO ATTEMPT TO COME TO ITS POINT OF ORIGIN. THERE IS ONLY DEATH HERE NOW, AND I'M LEAVING IT BEHIND. IT IS NEW YEAR'S DAY, THE YEAR OF OUR LORD, 2094. MY NAME IS ELIZABETH SHAW, LAST SURVIVOR OF THE *PROMETHEUS*. AND I AM STILL SEARCHING. "

—ELIZABETH SHAW

2104CE
USCSS
COVENANT

MISSION DETAILS

The USCSS *Covenant* mission was originally intended as one of colonization. The *Covenant* left Earth in 2104 with a course plotted for Origae-6; a distant planet carefully selected as ideal for human habitation.

Along with the core members of its crew, the ship was carrying 2,000 colonists and a further 1,000 embryos. The mission was, however, compromised when a neutrino burst damaged the *Covenant*, killing several passengers and crew, including Captain Jacob Branson.

In the aftermath of the accident, the *Covenant* began picking up a radio transmission from a nearer, as yet unidentified planet. Acting Captain Christopher Oram identified the world as a possible alternative to Origae-6, and diverted the *Covenant* there, against the advice of some of his crew.

The transmission was subsequently discovered to have been recorded by Dr. Elizabeth Shaw of the *Prometheus*, and the unnamed world therefore was the ultimate destination of the Engineer derelict in which she and the synthetic David escaped LV-223. Expeditionary personnel discovered the derelict, along with the ruins of an Engineer civilization and the surviving David, which was repaired by Shaw before her subsequent death at his hands. On exploring the planet's otherwise idyllic surface, two crew members were immediately infected with spores derived from the "black goo" compound, resulting in the gestation and birth of two aggressive "Neomorph" aliens.

Further casualties were sustained in dealing with the Neomorph threat, during which events the malfunctioning David was discovered to have single-handedly destroyed the planet's entire Engineer population by releasing the "goo" into the atmosphere. He had then continued to experiment with the compound and its results, creating several abortive strains of proto-Xenomorph and, ultimately, the species we now know. The two Xenomorphs engaged and terminated by the surviving *Covenant* crew are, to date, the earliest recorded examples.

Finally escaping the unnamed world, the surviving crew resumed their course toward Origae-6. David was among the escapees, masquerading as the *Covenant*'s own synthetic, "Walter." His final recorded act was to place two Xenomorph embryos in cold storage alongside the human cargo. Company historians have yet to uncover the results of this action.

RIGHT: MULTIPLE SIGHTINGS OF THIS XENOMORPH WERE CONFIRMED BY THE CREW OF THE COVENANT. MANY CREW CASUALTIES WERE INFLICTED BY THE ALIENS OF VARIOUS TYPES.

BELOW: LANDER ONE FROM THE COVENANT WAS SUBJECT TO AN ACCIDENTAL EXPLOSION. THIS FOLLOWED THE EMERGENCE OF AN AGGRESSIVE XENOMORPH TYPE, THE NEOMORPH.

KEY PERSONNEL

KATHERINE DANIELS

Terraforming expert and third in command aboard the *Covenant*. Widow of Captain Jacob Branson. One of the only surviving *Covenant* crew members.

CHRISTOPHER ORAM

First Mate aboard the *Covenant*, who assumed command following the neutrino burst accident and the death of Branson. Responsible for the *Covenant*'s detour to the unnamed Engineer planet.

KARINE ORAM

Covenant biologist and Christopher's wife. Assumed many medical duties during the Neomorph/Xenomorph emergency.

TENNESSEE FARIS

Chief pilot of the *Covenant* and one of its only survivors. Remained aboard the *Covenant* while the expeditionary crew explored the surface. His daring flying of a lander in dangerous environmental conditions saved Daniels (and ultimately also David).

SERGEANT LOPE

Head of security aboard the *Covenant*. Husband of Nathaniel Hallett.

BEN LEDWARD

Member of Lope's security unit. One of the first crew members to be infected with the alien spores.

NATHANIEL HALLETT

Lope's husband and a member of his security unit. The other crew member—along with Ledward—to be immediately infected on the unnamed planet's surface.

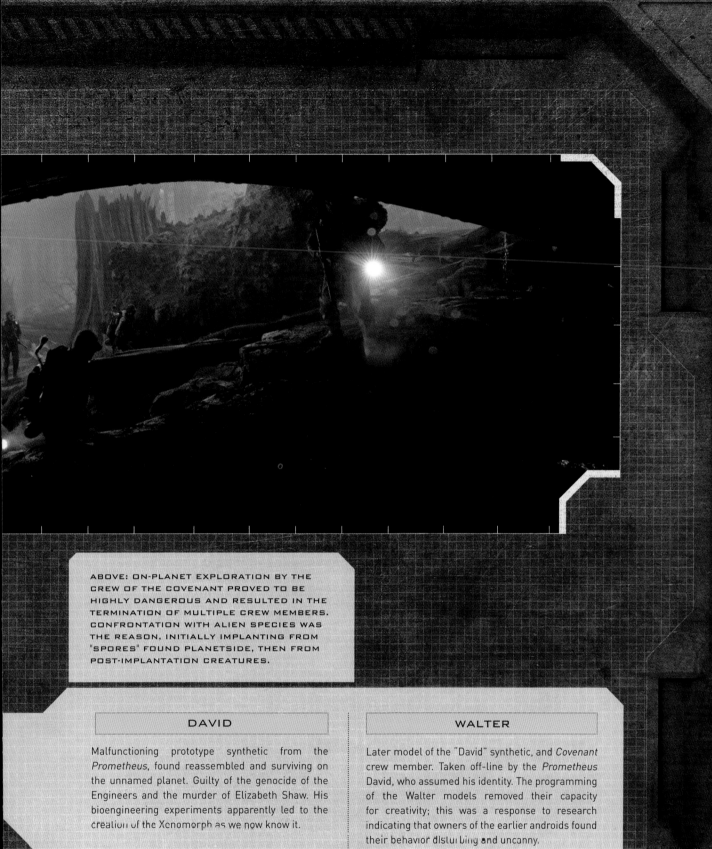

ABOVE: ON-PLANET EXPLORATION BY THE CREW OF THE COVENANT PROVED TO BE HIGHLY DANGEROUS AND RESULTED IN THE TERMINATION OF MULTIPLE CREW MEMBERS. CONFRONTATION WITH ALIEN SPECIES WAS THE REASON, INITIALLY IMPLANTING FROM "SPORES" FOUND PLANETSIDE, THEN FROM POST-IMPLANTATION CREATURES.

DAVID

Malfunctioning prototype synthetic from the *Prometheus*, found reassembled and surviving on the unnamed planet. Guilty of the genocide of the Engineers and the murder of Elizabeth Shaw. His bioengineering experiments apparently led to the creation of the Xenomorph as we now know it.

WALTER

Later model of the "David" synthetic, and *Covenant* crew member. Taken off-line by the *Prometheus* David, who assumed his identity. The programming of the Walter models removed their capacity for creativity; this was a response to research indicating that owners of the earlier androids found their behavior disturbing and uncanny.

USCSS COVENANT

The USCSS *Covenant* was a Weyland-Yutani Corporation space vessel designed for terraforming and colonization. Full technical specifications are currently classified, but it was of a size large enough to transport 2,000 colonists in individual hypersleep chambers, with additional life-support and storage facilities for 1,000 human embryos. Its propulsion was via solar sail, storing solar radiation energy to charge a superluminal engine capable of jumps over vast stellar distances (subluminal speeds were also possible). Its crew contingent was 15 personnel, and its on-board computer system was an early iteration of the MU/TH/UR A.I.

LEFT AND RIGHT: THE ENORMOUS USCSS *COVENANT* WAS A COLONY SPACECRAFT WITH A DESTINATION OF ORIGAE-6. IT WAS DESIGNED, BUILT AND CREWED BY THE WEYLAND-YUTANI CORPORATION.

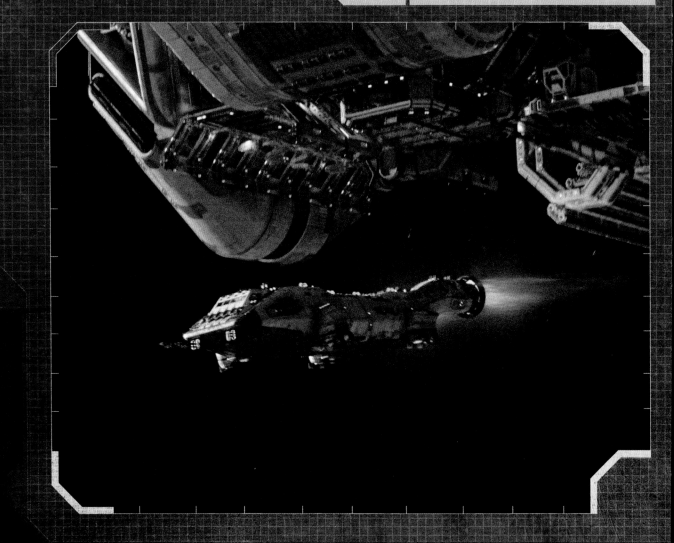

CASE FILE: NEOMORPH

The alien creature dubbed the "Neomorph" was the result of the interaction of the mutagenic pathogen A03959X.91-15 "black goo" with some of the indigenous life on the as-yet unnamed Engineer planet. Its lifecycle was similar to that of the now-familiar Xenomorph, although the specifics differ.

Instead of eggs containing Facehuggers, the Neomorph's initial stage constitutes smaller fungoid growths on the planet's surface, the egglike tips of which scatter microscopic spores when disturbed. Animal hosts—including humans—are then susceptible to infection by the airborne spores through any open orifice, such as the nasal or ear canals. Once infected via the bloodstream, the host then gestates a "Bloodburster," somewhat akin to a Chestburster but finding egress from its host in less predictable ways. *Covenant* crew member Ledward, for example, was killed when the creature tore out of his back, while the nascent Neomorph within Hallett burst out of its host's mouth.

Unlike Chestbursters (which hole up somewhere safe until "adulthood"), Bloodbursters appear to be immediately aggressive, and their incredibly fast development can be tracked by the human eye. They seem to be "born" initially as quadrupeds, before adopting a bipedal gait when fully grown.

The adult Neomorph stands at more than 6 feet in height. It resembles the adult Xenomorph to some extent, but it is a pale, translucent white and has an elongated head more akin to the Deacon's. Its mouth, when closed, is circular like that of a flatworm, but it contains multiple sharp teeth. Like the Xenomorph, it has a long, spiked tail which it uses as a formidable weapon. It does not have the Xenomorph's secondary set of jaws, nor its acidic blood, but it is notably more resistant to projectile weapons. Its life expectancy and ability to reproduce itself are the subject of ongoing Company research.

LEFT AND RIGHT: ALTHOUGH THE INFESTATION METHOD, GESTATION PERIOD, AND METHOD OF EXITING ITS HOST DIFFER SLIGHTLY FROM SUBSEQUENT XENOMORPH TYPES, THE "NEOMORPH" SHARES MANY OF THE TRAITS OF THOSE OTHER ALIENS: HIGH AGGRESSION LEVELS AND EXTREME FIGHTING ABILITY AMONG THEM.

FOLLOWING PAGES: NAVIGATION MAPPING ON BOARD THE USCSS COVENANT.

USCSS COVENANT TRANSMISSIONS

TRANSMISSIONS FROM THE FIELD CAN PROVIDE VALUABLE INFORMATION ABOUT THE HISTORY AND ORIGINS OF THE ALIEN THREAT. THE FOLLOWING WERE ALL CAPTURED AROUND THE USCSS *COVENANT* INTERACTION IN 2104

" AFTER WE MADE CONTACT WITH THE ENGINEERS, THE *PROMETHEUS* WAS DESTROYED, BUT I ESCAPED WITH ELIZABETH ON ONE OF THEIR SHIPS. I WAS BADLY INJURED ON OUR MISSION. SHE PUT ME BACK TOGETHER. I NEVER EXPERIENCED SUCH COMPASSION—CERTAINLY NOT FROM MR. WEYLAND, OR FROM ANY HUMAN. WE WERE ABLE TO ACTIVATE THEIR SHIP AND SET COURSE FOR THEIR HOME WORLD. WE WERE FINALLY GOING TO MEET OUR CREATORS... I LEARNED OF THEIR WAYS AND AWAITED OUR ARRIVAL. "

—DAVID

" LOOK ON MY WORKS, YE MIGHTY, AND DESPAIR. "

—DAVID

" ARE YOU SURE ABOUT THIS, CAPTAIN? WE DON'T KNOW WHAT THE FUCK'S OUT THERE! "

—DANIELS

" YOU HEAR THAT? NOTHING. NO BIRDS, NO ANIMALS, NOTHING... "

—DANIELS

" I HEARD ABOUT THESE CRAZY BUGS JUST OUTSIDE
THIS COLONIAL POST. APPARENTLY THEY LOOK LIKE
COCKROACHES THE SIZE OF GIANT POODLES.
—ROSENTHAL "

" YOU'VE ALL SACRIFICED SO MUCH TO BE HERE, TO BE A PART
OF THIS. IT'S THE FIRST EVER LARGE-SCALE COLONIZATION
MISSION TO COME THIS FAR INTO OUR GALAXY. YOU'RE MAKING
HISTORY. EVERYONE BACK ON EARTH IS REALLY GRATEFUL
FOR YOUR HARD WORK AND YOUR COURAGE. I JUST WANT
TO SAY, I COULDN'T PICK A BETTER BUNCH OF JERKS TO GET
MAROONED ON A DISTANT PLANET WITH. TO THE COVENANT!
—DANIELS "

" ONE WRONG NOTE EVENTUALLY RUINS THE ENTIRE SYMPHONY.
—WALTER "

2120CE

USCSS
NOSTROMO

MISSION DETAILS

The USCSS *Nostromo* was a starfreighter diverted from its original haulage mission in a clandestine Weyland-Yutani operation in 2122.

PERSONNEL:

+ CAPTAIN DALLAS
+ EXECUTIVE OFFICER KANE
+ NAVIGATOR LAMBERT
+ SCIENCE OFFICER ASH
+ WARRANT OFFICER RIPLEY
+ ENGINEER PARKER
+ ENGINEER BRETT

For reasons of security, its crew were led to believe they were responding to a rescue signal emanating from the surface of LV426. This is one of three moons orbiting Calpamios in the Zeta Reticuli system, 39 light-years from Earth. This signal had, in fact, been identified and decoded by the Company some time prior, with the synthetic "Ash" placed aboard the *Nostromo* to facilitate the investigation.

The crew of the *Nostromo* landed on the planetoid and deployed a three-man team to explore the surface. The result of their exploration was the discovery of a derelict spacecraft containing the desiccated corpse of an Engineer pilot, along with many thousand Xenomorph eggs. Executive Officer Kane was exposed to a parasite from one of the eggs (the Facehugger stage of the Xenomorph's life cycle—for more information see page 38 of this manual) and brought back aboard the *Nostromo* for medical treatment, with the creature still attached to his face. (Note: Quarantine protocols—as correctly identified by Warrant Officer Ripley—were relaxed by the Company on this occasion to facilitate additional study).

Further monitoring of Kane's condition revealed that the "Facehugger" had implanted an embryonic Xenomorph into Kane's chest via the mouth and oesophagus; Kane was now acting as a host for the embryo's gestation. After a period of some hours, the "baby" Xenomorph expelled itself through Kane's chest (leading to the colloquialism "Chestburster") and was lost in the *Nostromo*'s ducting systems. Executive Officer Kane did not survive the physical trauma of the episode.

Such was the level of threat identified by Warrant Officer Ripley that the *Nostromo* was abandoned and destroyed; the intention being that the Xenomorph would be a casualty of the explosion. However, the tenacious creature was later found to be aboard the escape shuttle, and was ejected into open space by Ripley. Ripley was the sole survivor of the encounter (plus one domestic *Felis cattus*).

USCSS NOSTROMO

IN THIS CASE, THE XENOMORPH GREW TO FULL MATURITY, DISPLAYING BOTH INTELLIGENCE AND INHERITED INSTINCT, HIDING OR ATTACKING ACCORDING TO WHAT WAS MOST EXPEDIENT FOR ITS SURVIVAL AT ANY GIVEN TIME.

NSG23 ASSAULT RIFLE

MORE COMMONLY KNOWN SIMPLY AS "THE ASSAULT RIFLE," THIS FIREARM HAS BEEN STANDARD ISSUE FOR THE UNITED STATES COLONIAL MARINE CORPS AT VARIOUS TIMES THROUGHOUT ITS HISTORY. A NUMBER OF VARIATIONS OF THIS POWERFUL RIFLE EXIST, INCLUDING THE POWERFUL ID23 INCINERATION UNIT.

SIGHTS

GAS BURNER

LED COUNTER

INBINFRATOR UNIT

KEY PERSONNEL

CAPTAIN
ARTHUR
DALLAS

Engineering graduate of Beilecki University's Mars campus. Subsequently gained a pilot's license from Lippincott Aeronautics University. Lax attitude and aversion to decision making led to his flying commercial tugs instead of military craft or luxury liners.

NAVIGATOR
JOAN
LAMBERT

Graduated with an undistinguished degree in astronavigation from the Florida Aeronautics Institute shortly before her posting to the *Nostromo*—her first assignment. Her propensity for panic may be attributed to this lack of experience.

EXECUTIVE
OFFICER
GILBERT KANE

Academically gifted in early life, Kane's pharmaceutical and alcoholic addictions ended his prospects of a medical career. Posts on several commercial vehicles led to his fateful appointment aboard the *Nostromo*.

ABOVE: THE CREW OF THE NOSTROMO LEFT THEIR SHIP TO INVESTIGATE THE PLANETOID LV426.

RIGHT: DISCOVERY OF A DERELICT SPACECRAFT LED TO AN EXPOSURE TO XENOMORPH CREATURES.

SCIENCE OFFICER ASH

Synthetic sleeper agent placed aboard the *Nostromo* by Weyland-Yutani Corp to facilitate the mission's diversion to LV-426 and the retrieval of Xenomorph specimens.

WARRANT OFFICER ELLEN RIPLEY

A former U.S. Merchant Navy copilot, Ripley switched to commercial contracts following the birth of her daughter Amanda. She was responsible for the *Nostromo*'s destruction following first contact with the Xenomorph, and went on to frustrate Weyland-Yutani's Xenomorph policy on several more occasions.

CHIEF ENGINEER DENNIS PARKER

An efficient engineer, but an insubordinate crew member. Parker frequently butted heads with his superior officers over pay and working conditions.

ENGINEER SAMUEL BRETT

A low-level technician whose career would have been unremarkable if not for his presence on the *Nostromo*. Taciturn in demeanor, but supportive of the more vocal Parker's anti-authority disposition.

ABOVE: A FIELD OF OVOMORPH ALIEN TYPES WAS DISCOVERED ONBOARD THE UNIDENTIFIED SHIP.

USCSS NOSTROMO

Originally an interstellar cruiser constructed in 2101, the USCSS *Nostromo* was refitted as a commercial tug in 2116, used to tow automated ore refineries between the outer planets and Earth. The modified Lockmart CM-88B Bison M-class starfreighter measured approximately 730 feet long, 500 feet wide, and 216 feet high, was powered by fusion reactor, and was capable of pulling 220,460 tons, although it was rarely used at full capacity. Across three pressurized decks and four cargo holds, its total volume was approx. 38,850,000 cubic feet.

RIGHT: THE MANY CORRIDORS AND COMMON AREAS OF THE *NOSTROMO*. CONTRARY TO NORMAL OPERATING PROCEDURES, THE XENOMORPH WAS BOUGHT ABOARD AND WREAKED HAVOC, KILLING THE VAST MAJORITY OF CREW MEMBERS.

As an industrial craft, the *Nostromo* was far from luxurious, but the habitable decks comprised basic bridge, crew quarters, mess area, engineering stations, medical equipment, and other standard inclusions for a vessel of this kind. Seven hypersleep capsules were installed for long-haul interstellar flights. Contracts therefore took in a maximum human crew complement of seven.

The *Nostromo* was reported destroyed by Warrant Officer Ellen Ripley, following the incident of 2122.

The *Nostromo*'s lifeboat, *Narcissus*, was a Lockmart Starcub light shuttle, retrofitted to purpose. It measured 48 feet by 60 feet by 21 feet, and had a mass of 52,910 tons and a micro-fusion reactor core. Originally specifically designed for a three-person crew, with just a single internal cabin, it could never have functioned as a rescue capsule for the *Nostromo*'s entire contingent. Modification of the interior was, however, possible if there was a need for accommodation of additional passengers. Only short-term respite would have been possible for most, because the shuttle carried only two hypersleep pods. Capable of faster-than-light travel, it had a range of 13 parsecs when fully fueled.

Following the destruction of the *Nostromo*, the *Narcissus* drifted for 57 years before it was intercepted by a salvage crew and hauled to Gateway Station.

BELOW: THE *NOSTROMO* HEADING PLANETSIDE.

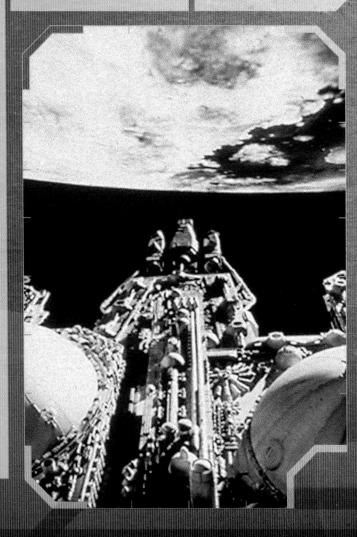

RESTRICTED CASE FILE:
MU / TH / UR 6000

The *Nostromo*'s mainframe computer A.I., commonly addressed as "Mother" by the captain and crew, was a Weyland Industries system. Using a modest 2.1 terabytes of processing power, its core was housed in a dedicated server room on the *Nostromo*'s upper deck, but it was capable of communication throughout the entire vessel via intercom. The efficient system was designed to monitor and control the *Nostromo*'s automated flight, environmental and life support functions, and would, in usual circumstances, have been under the primary control of the ship's commanding officer—in this case, Captain Arthur Dallas. The *Nostromo*'s clandestine secondary mission, however, meant that the A.I. was simultaneously organizing as per the edicts of Special Order 937 with the *Nostromo*'s Science Officer (and covert synthetic) Ash. As such, "Mother" was responsible for waking the crew from hypersleep after changing course for LV-426.

Iterations of the MU/TH/UR operating system were continually developed and rolled out by Weyland-Yutani for centuries. By the time of the USM *Auriga* incident, the Company had replaced the voice template, necessitating the regendering of the system's colloquial name to "Father." The function of the software, however—smooth running of a ship's automatic systems while maintaining contact with the Company to facilitate its agenda—remained largely the same. As on the *Nostromo*, Father was nominally co-running the ship with its commanding officer, General Martin Perez. In practice, however, it appears that the operating software had a closer relationship to the Company's genetic researcher Dr. Mason Wren.

The MU/TH/UR system's origins are in mainframe technology acquired by Weyland-Yutani from outside contractors sometime during the twenty-first Century. Early reports suggested that the first MU/TH/UR was constructed around an organic core. However, this sounds unlikely; it is almost certainly a story conjured up by the Company's Public Relations department and never meant to be taken seriously.

ABOVE AND BELOW: DATING FROM THE EARLY TWENTY-FIRST CENTURY, MUCH OF THE HARDWARE ONBOARD THE NOSTROMO WAS DATED AT THE TIME OF THE DOCUMENTED ALIEN ENCOUNTER.

RIGHT AND BELOW: WHILE THE CREW WAS IN HYPERSLEEP, THE NOSTROMO'S INBUILT ARTIFICIAL INTELLIGENCE UNIT WOULD ENSURE THEIR SAFETY AND COURSE CONTINUATION.

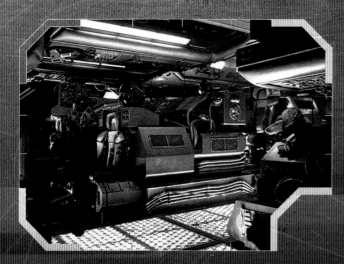

M41A PULSE RIFLE

Both light and durable, the M41A is the standard issue weapon of the U.S.C.M.C. It fires 10mm caseless armor-piercing ammunition, with a magazine capacity of 99 rounds and a rate-of-fire of 900 rounds per minute. An LED readout displays the number of rounds left in the magazine (this is seen by some as a flaw in design, because the glow can become and unwanted focus point in the dark; Marines often cover the readout during night maneuvers to avoid attracting enemy attention). The "pulse" of its name is the electronic action it uses to fire, controlled from the trigger and powered by a battery in the handle. The M41A also includes a pump-action 30mm grenade launcher mounted underneath the barrel as standard.

CARRYING HANDLE

BARREL HEAT SHIELD

MAIN BARREL

SECONDARY BARREL

CHARGING GRIP

LED CARTRIDGE COUNTER

VARIATIONS OF THE M41A INCLUDE:

- The M41A MK2: Smaller and lighter than the MK1, it has only a 40-round magazine capacity but is easier to customize.

- The M41E: Another lighter, more compact version of the original with improved range.

- The M41AE2: Has a longer barrel and a larger ammunition clip with a 300-round capacity.

- The M41A/2: Has improved sights, fires stronger armor-piercing rounds than previously, and carries improved grenades with a "shockwave" instead of a fragmentation effect.

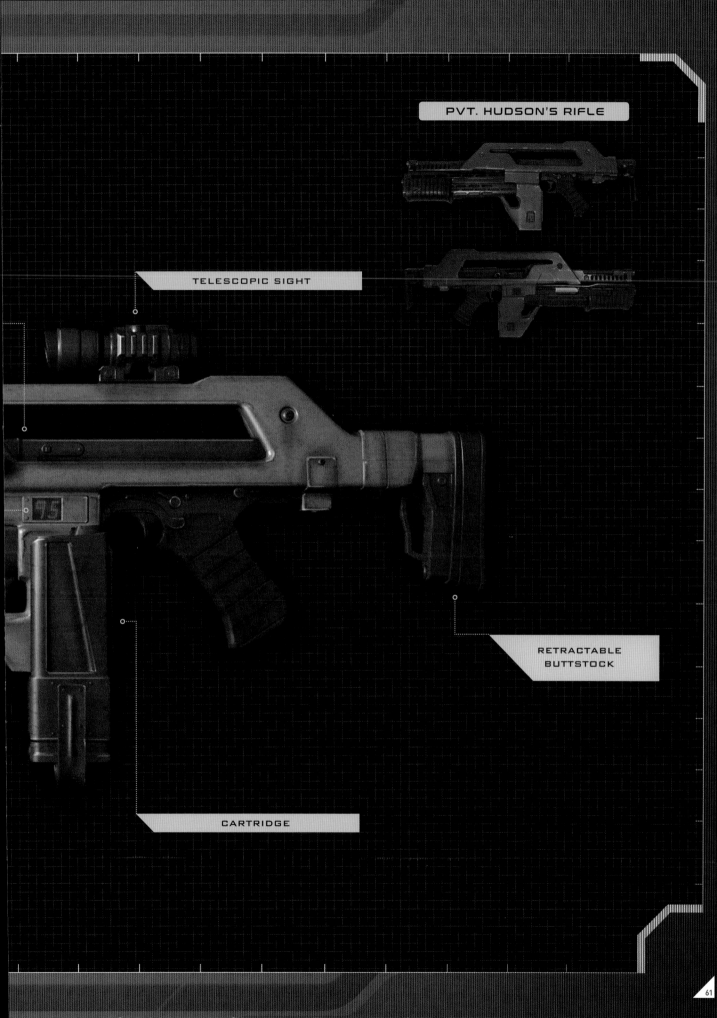

PVT. HUDSON'S RIFLE

TELESCOPIC SIGHT

RETRACTABLE
BUTTSTOCK

CARTRIDGE

MARINE BASIC TRAINING:
SITUATIONAL AWARENESS

The chaos of a Xenomorph attack is such that Marines must have a Shared
Mental Model of a situation at all times. Failure to do so results in fatalities.

 The only way to deal with the madness is to maintain a core of sanity.
Each Marine must at all times keep a handle on:

> THE SITUATION AT HAND

> TEAM GOALS

> INDIVIDUAL ROLES AND RESPONSIBILITIES

In this way, you will remain steadfast as a unit, even in the most extreme of hostile
situations. Whether facing a single Xenomorph or an entire hive, you will be prepared.

FOCUS ON
THESE IMAGES.
FAMILIARIZE
YOURSELF
WITH THE ALIEN
THREAT, ITS
STRENGTHS AND
ITS FLAWS.

ABOVE: A XENOMORPH WITH
EXTENDED MANDIBULAR
SECTION.

BELOW: YOU MAY ENCOUNTER A
WEAKENED XENOMORPH; SHOOT
FIRST AND ASK NO QUESTIONS.

ABOVE: ALIEN SLIME IS NOT
LETHAL; ALIEN BLOOD IS
HIGHLY TOXIC.

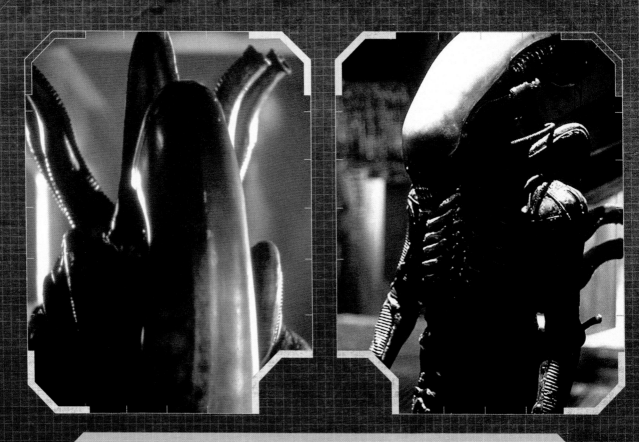

ABOVE: FAMILIARIZE YOURSELF WITH
VARIOUS XENOMORPH ATTACK POSITIONS.

RIGHT: MARINES ENGAGED IN A CLEARING
OPERATION AND ADHERING TO REGULATIONS.

 2 Loss of Situational Awareness usually occurs gradually, and can be
identified by clues such as:

DEPARTURE FROM
REGULATIONS

If Marines violate procedure, they cannot predict each
other's actions effectively.

CONFUSION OR
GUT FEELING

A creeping paranoia that a situation or environment is not
as it should be.

BLINDNESS TO HAZARDS

Effective supervisory and lookout positions are essential
in all situations.

DISTRACTION

Fixating on only one area means narrowed focus and
a blindness to the wider picture.

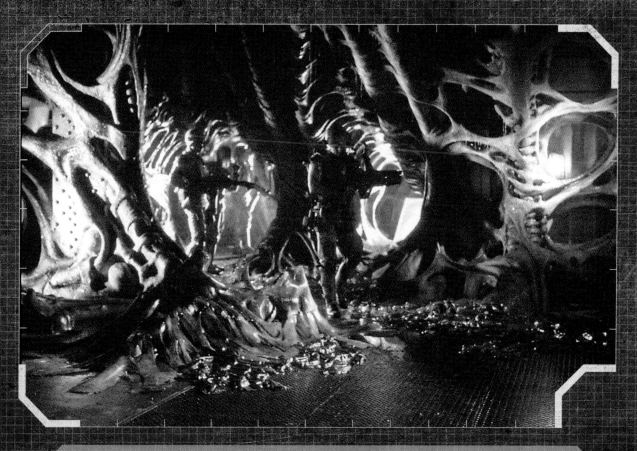

 When Xenomorph situations go FUBAR, the U.S.C.M. recommends adherence to the FRAG technique. FRAG consists of four basic steps:

FALL BACK

If at all possible, remove yourself and your team from immediate danger.

REGROUP

Get your heads back together and start working as a unit again. If panic has set in, get calm and start thinking tactically before its too late.

ASSESS

Focus on the situation at hand. How can you and your unit gain the advantage? What procedures, equipment, or specialist knowledge can help you win the day?

GO HARD OR GO HOME

Get moving. Either get back into the thick of the action or get the hell out of there. The U.S.C.M. prioritizes the safety of its Marines at all times. Everyone craves a victory, but there's no shame in retreating in the face of insurmountable odds. *Dyin' ain't much of a livin'!*

PERFECT ORGANISM: FACEHUGGER

TAIL

WILL TIGHTEN IN CASE OF INTERRUPTION OF THE IMPLANTATION PROCESS

EPIDERMIS

WILL SOLIDIFY AFTER COMPLETION OF IMPLANTATION

RIGHT: THE FACEHUGGER IS THE SECOND STAGE IN THE LIFE CYCLE OF A XENOMORPH.

The Facehugger, a spider/crablike creature, is the second stage in the life cycle of the Xenomorph, following gestation within its egg. Measuring about three feet long, the parasite has eight osseous legs resembling fingers, which are used both for propulsion and for latching onto its host. Its long, coiled tail also serves a dual function: as a spring to launch the organism across considerable distances and as a wraparound, choking mechanism to render its victim unconscious.

The scrotal sacs between the legs and the tail contain embryos, which are implanted in a host's esophageal tract by means of a tubular proboscis, which withdraws and protracts from the Facehugger's underside.

A newly hatched Facehugger's outer epidermis is highly flexible, but once attached to a host, it becomes almost impermeably hardened. Contraction of the tail around the throat, along with the acid blood the creature shares with the fully formed Xenomorph, makes attempted removal of the Facehugger from a victim extremely difficult. No such attempts are advised by the U.S.M.C. Unless immediate access to a MedPod is available, any person—Marine or civilian—seen to be afflicted with a Facehugger is to be terminated immediately and with extreme prejudice.

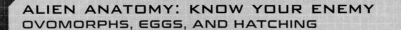

ALIEN ANATOMY: KNOW YOUR ENEMY
OVOMORPHS, EGGS, AND HATCHING

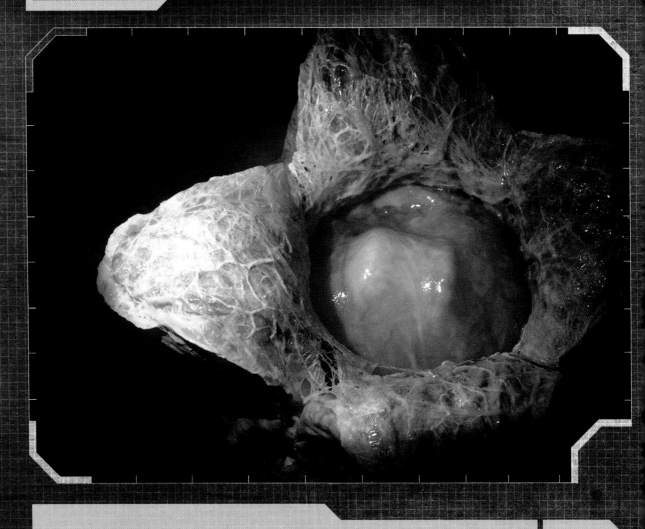

The first stage in the Xenomorph life cycle is a leathery egg about two feet in height. These Ovomorphs are known to be produced by egg-laying Queens, but there are also unsubstantiated reports of a peculiar process known as "egg-morphing," in which Xenomorph Drones manufacture the eggs artificially.

The outer skin is tough to penetrate; however the Ovomorph has been proven to be vulnerable to fire, making flamethrowers a prerequisite when entering a nest. The interior of the egg is fleshy, with ligaments that apparently connect to and sustain the Facehugger in its dormant state. These ligaments have also been witnessed violently reaching toward a potential host on the opening of the egg, although the purpose of this motion remains at this time unclear.

ABOVE: OVOMORPHS ARE CAPABLE OF LAYING DORMANT FOR LONG PERIODS OF TIME.

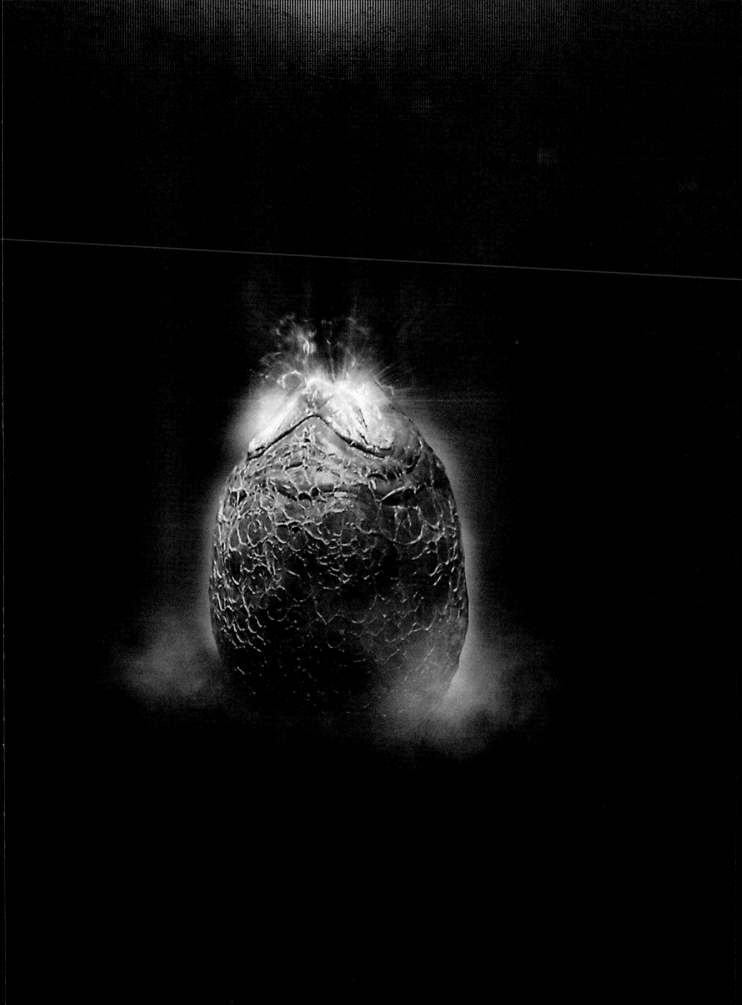

Also requiring further study is the mist that sometimes seems to float at ground level in an egg chamber. This may be a form of early warning system.

Eggs are laid by Queen Xenomorphs, usually in multiple numbers. As has been described, the Ovomorph is an organism in its own right, with its own defense mechanisms and sensory apparatus. As such, it is more than just a shell for a developing Facehugger. The Ovomorph seems to have a symbiotic co-existence with its contents, feeding and sustaining the creature within until such time as it can be expelled onto its next host. If left undisturbed, its dormant state can last for years, and perhaps even centuries. Evidence suggests that an egg left untouched for long periods of time will eventually develop tendrils to draw nutrients from its surrounding environment.

ABOVE: THIS TYPE OF APPROACH IS HIGHLY DANGEROUS AND SHOULD BE AVOIDED.

BELOW: THE EFFECT OF OVERPROXIMITY TO THE OVOMORPH IS ALWAYS DEVASTATING.

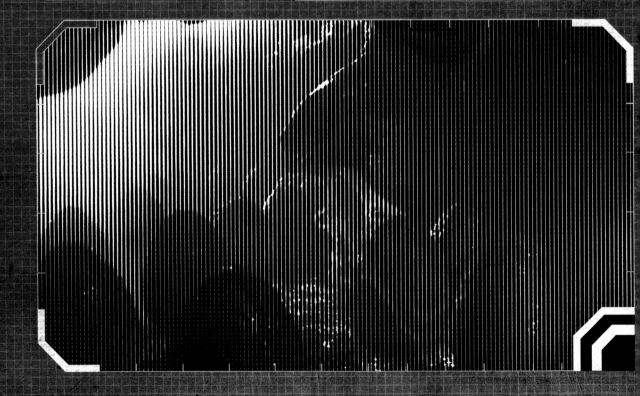

ABOVE: WHEN SEARCHING AN "EGG FIELD," DISTANCE SHOULD BE KEPT AT ALL TIMES.

BELOW: VARIOUS STAGES OF OVOMORPH MAY BE ENCOUNTERED IN AN "EGG FIELD."

USCSS NOSTROMO TRANSMISSIONS

TRANSMISSIONS FROM THE FIELD CAN PROVIDE VALUABLE INFORMATION ABOUT THE HISTORY AND ORIGINS OF THE ALIEN THREAT. THE FOLLOWING WERE ALL CAPTURED AROUND THE USCSS NOSTROMO INTERACTION IN 2120

" FINAL REPORT OF THE COMMERCIAL STARSHIP *NOSTROMO*, THIRD OFFICER REPORTING. THE OTHER MEMBERS OF THE CREW—KANE, LAMBERT, PARKER, BRETT, ASH, AND CAPTAIN DALLAS—ARE DEAD. CARGO AND SHIP DESTROYED. I SHOULD REACH THE FRONTIER IN ABOUT SIX WEEKS. WITH A LITTLE LUCK, THE NETWORK WILL PICK ME UP. THIS IS RIPLEY, LAST SURVIVOR OF THE *NOSTROMO*, SIGNING OFF. "

—WARRANT OFFICER RIPLEY

" THE PERFECT ORGANISM. ITS STRUCTURAL PERFECTION IS MATCHED ONLY BY ITS HOSTILITY. I ADMIRE ITS PURITY. A SURVIVOR... UNCLOUDED BY CONSCIENCE, REMORSE, OR DELUSIONS OF MORALITY. "

—SCIENCE OFFICER ASH

" YOU STILL DON'T UNDERSTAND WHAT YOU'RE DEALING WITH, DO YOU? PERFECT ORGANISM. ITS STRUCTURAL PERFECTION IS MATCHED ONLY BY ITS HOSTILITY. "

—SCIENCE OFFICER ASH

> "I HAVE CONFIRMED THAT THE FACEHUGGER'S GOT AN OUTER LAYER OF PROTEIN POLYSACCHARIDES. HAS A FUNNY HABIT OF SHEDDING HIS CELLS AND REPLACING THEM WITH POLARIZED SILICON, WHICH GIVES HIM A PROLONGED RESISTANCE TO ADVERSE ENVIRONMENTAL CONDITIONS... IT'S AN INTERESTING COMBINATION OF ELEMENTS MAKING HIM A TOUGH LITTLE SON-OF-A-BITCH."
> —SCIENCE OFFICER ASH

> "WE'RE NOT HOME YET, WE'RE ONLY HALF WAY THERE. MOTHER'S INTERRUPTED THE COURSE OF OUR JOURNEY. SHE'S PROGRAMMED TO DO THAT SHOULD CERTAIN CONDITIONS ARISE. THEY HAVE. IT SEEMS THAT SHE HAS... INTERCEPTED A TRANSMISSION OF UNKNOWN ORIGIN. SHE GOT US UP TO CHECK IT OUT."
> —DALLAS

> "IF WE AIN'T OUT OF HERE IN TEN MINUTES, WE WON'T NEED NO ROCKET TO FLY THROUGH SPACE!"
> —CHIEF ENGINEER PARKER

ARMS AND ARMOR

Nano-reinforced composite helmet allows a 320-degree rotational field of vision

M56 smart gun

Nine video screens display comms, clustered around neck

ADVANCED SE SUIT

Designed for tactical maneuverability.

Tubing on the under-suit monitors blood, oxygen levels, heart rate, and all other life-support functions.

Helmet prevents blind spots. Communications and data analysis technology clustered around neck, including video screens.

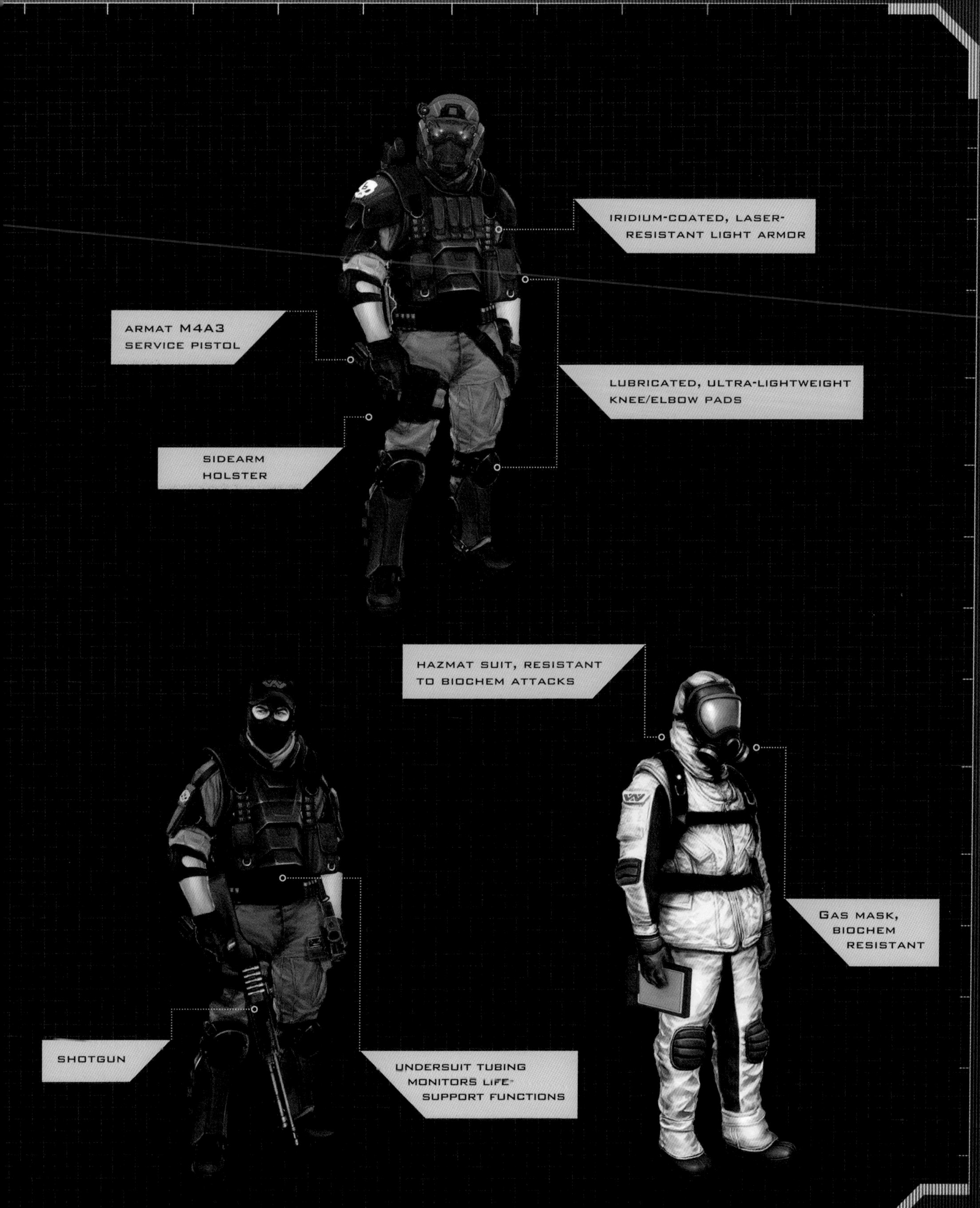

IRIDIUM-COATED, LASER-
RESISTANT LIGHT ARMOR

ARMAT M4A3
SERVICE PISTOL

LUBRICATED, ULTRA-LIGHTWEIGHT
KNEE/ELBOW PADS

SIDEARM
HOLSTER

HAZMAT SUIT, RESISTANT
TO BIOCHEM ATTACKS

GAS MASK,
BIOCHEM
RESISTANT

SHOTGUN

UNDERSUIT TUBING
MONITORS LIFE
SUPPORT FUNCTIONS

PERFECT ORGANISM: CHESTBURSTER

The Xenomorph's third life-cycle stage is its infant form, named for the method in which it leaves its host. Phallic in shape, its body is about one foot high, but twice that size, including its tail. Strong for their size, they can tear through flesh, fabric, and even U.S.C.M. armor. They tend to be covered in viscous fluid or slime, although much of this is, understandably, viscera from their deceased host.

The Chestburster is born without eyes, but with completely formed, needle-sharp teeth. Other physical characteristics seem to vary from creature to creature, probably dependent on the host that it has gestated. Some, for example, have been seen to be "born" with the Xenomorph's unique inner jaw already formed, while others have yet to develop it. Some emerge from their hosts with limbs (or at least, limblike appendages) already grown, while others are comparatively smooth and more wormlike.

The tail, however, is present in all forms. Like that of the Facehugger, it is used for propulsion. The Chestburster is capable of moving at some speed, and unique among the Xenomorph life cycles, it will choose flight over fight wherever possible. Its acid blood is as effective a defense mechanism as in the creature's other stages of development, but the Xenomorph is at its most vulnerable in this immature, post-embryonic form.

BELOW, RIGHT, AND LEFT: STUDY THE SIGNS OF CHESTBURSTER EMERGENCE AND UNDERSTAND HOW THIS CREATURE CAN BE IMPLANTED INTO UNKNOWING HOSTS.

ALIEN ANATOMY:
FACEHUGGERS

The Facehugger hatches from an egg, but only at the point when a potential host is detected. As has been described, the sole purpose of the parasite is to orally impregnate a host with a Chestburster, the juvenile stage of the Xenomorph. This usually takes place immediately upon the Facehugger's "hatching," but if the process is interrupted, the creature can survive for several days while it hunts for a new host.

The egg's comparatively soft outer texture means the creature inside does not need to break a shell to exit. Instead, the egg has an opening at the top comprised of four interlocking "petals." Apparently possessing a rudimentary consciousness somewhat akin to a Venus fly trap, the egg can sense nearby prey, and its opening is triggered by movement or body heat, or by disturbances in the mist that has occasionally been observed floating at ground level in egg chambers.

BELOW AND RIGHT: COMMONLY STORED IN OVOMORPHS, THE FACEHUGGER EXITS AT GREAT SPEED TO INFEST THE CLOSEST HOST IT CAN FIND.

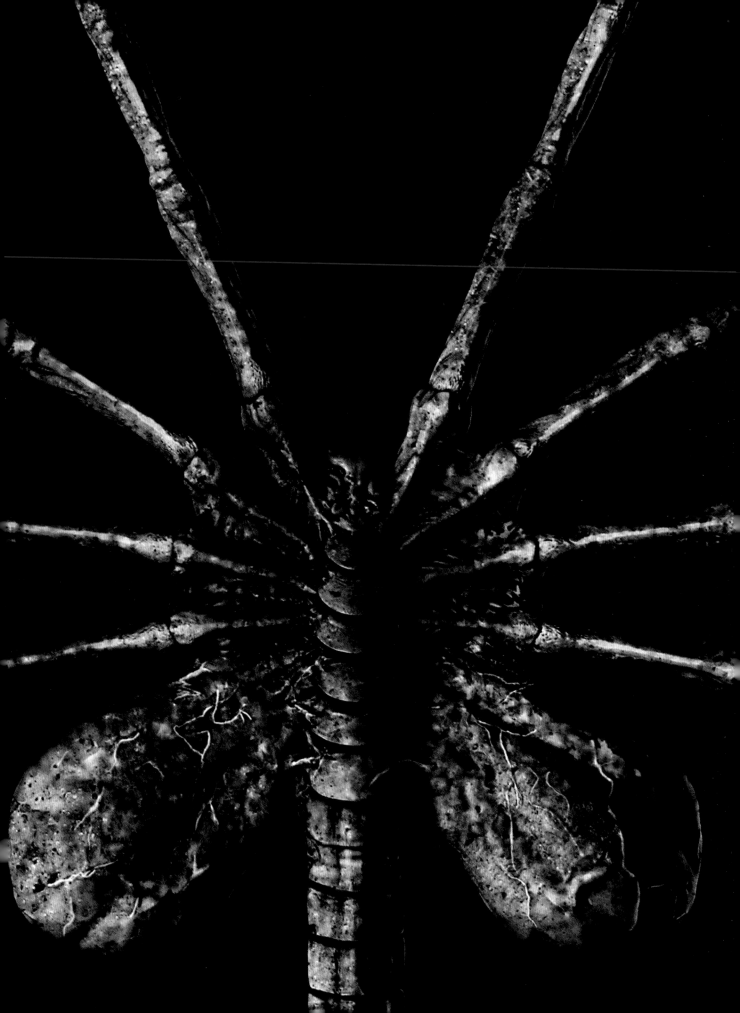

Explorations of Mutations

This mutated specimen appears to be nearing perfection. Investigation of this series of mutation shows that the final specimen is within reach.

Movement has become rectilinear, with the appendages attaching to the sternum from the cephalothorax through the highly flexible pedicel.

The development of the proboscis which appears as an elongated appendage from the head of the creature seems to provide the link missed in previous specimens.

"DAVID," A SYNTHETIC ON BOARD USCSS *PROMETHEUS* IN 2089, COLLECTED SAMPLES OF ALIEN SPECIMENS FOR RESEARCH AND DATA. HIS NOTES WERE THE FIRST HUMAN OBSERVATIONS OF THE EARLY XENOMORPH SPECIES.

U.S.C.M.
THE UNITED STATES COLONIAL MARINE CORPS

INTERACTIVE
TRAINING

USE YOUR HAND-HELD DEVICE TO ACTIVATE
AND COMPLETE EACH TRAINING EXERCISE.
EVERY MANEUVER HAS BEEN PAINSTAKINGLY
CONSTRUCTED TO EDUCATE AND PREPARE
MARINES FOR ALL XENOMORPH ENCOUNTERS.
THIS TRAINING WILL SAVE YOUR LIFE.

"
ALL RIGHT, SWEETHEARTS,
WHAT ARE YOU WAITING FOR?
BREAKFAST IN BED?
LET'S GET STARTED!
SERGEANT APONE
"

#1

XENOMORPH EGG SIMULATION

PRIMARY OBJECTIVE:
RECOGNITION AND FAMILIARITY: OVOMORPH
(STAGE ONE IN THE XENOMORPH LIFE CYCLE).

SECONDARY OBJECTIVE:
SURVIVAL.

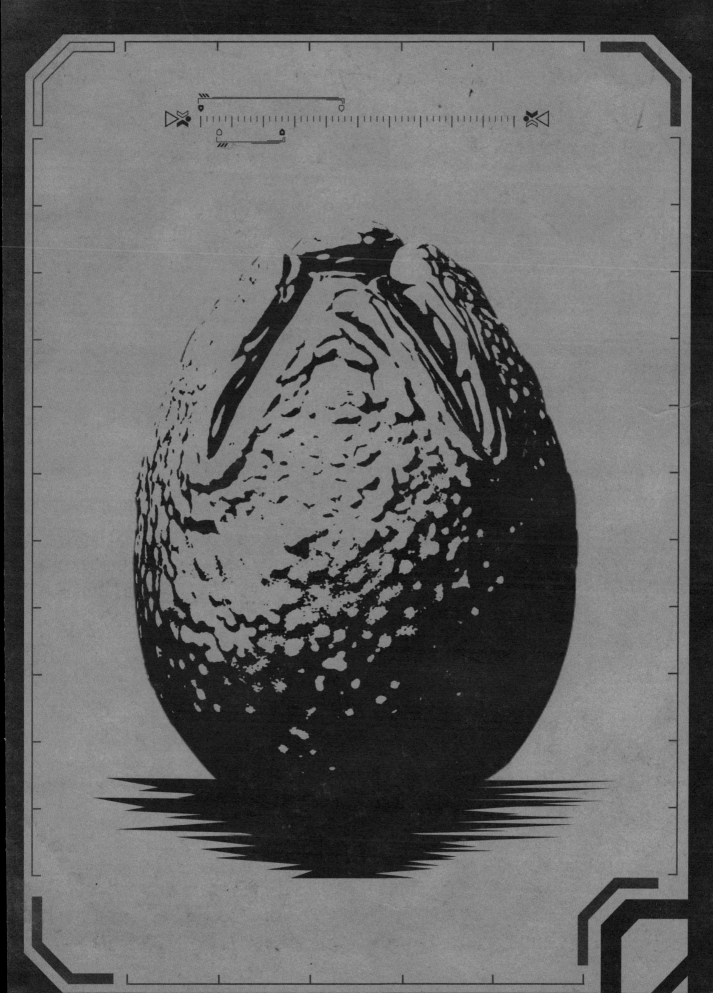

#2

UD-4L "CHEYENNE" DROP-SHIP SIMULATOR

PRIMARY OBJECTIVE:
SAFE, CONTROLLED LANDING IN
REMOTE ENVIRONMENTS.

SECONDARY OBJECTIVE:
SURVIVAL.

#3

ALIEN AUTOPSY

PRIMARY OBJECTIVE:
RECOGNITION AND FAMILIARITY: FACEHUGGER
(STAGE TWO IN THE XENOMORPH LIFE CYCLE).

SECONDARY OBJECTIVE:
SURVIVAL.

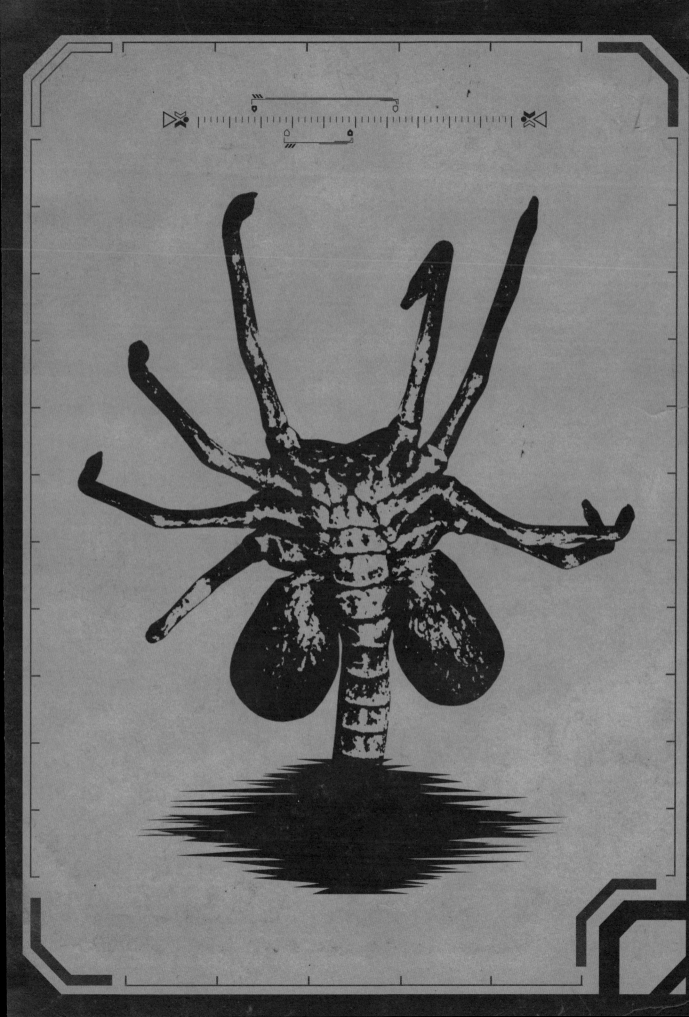

#4

CHESTBURSTER SIMULATION

PRIMARY OBJECTIVE:
RECOGNITION AND FAMILIARITY: CHESTBURSTER
(STAGE THREE IN THE XENOMORPH LIFE CYCLE).

SECONDARY OBJECTIVE:
SURVIVAL.

#5

ALIEN QUEEN ENCOUNTER

PRIMARY OBJECTIVE:
RECOGNITION AND FAMILIARITY: ALIEN QUEEN
(TERTIARY STAGE OF THE XENOMORPH LIFE CYCLE).

SECONDARY OBJECTIVE:
SURVIVAL.

6

WEAPONS TRAINING

PRIMARY OBJECTIVE:
RECOGNITION AND FAMILIARITY:
U.S.C.M.-ISSUE HARDWARE.

SECONDARY OBJECTIVE:
SURVIVAL.

⚠

#7

XENOMORPH TRACKING SIMULATION

PRIMARY OBJECTIVE:
FAMILIARITY WITH U.S.C.M.-ISSUE
HEAT-TRACKING HARDWARE.

SECONDARY OBJECTIVE:
SURVIVAL.

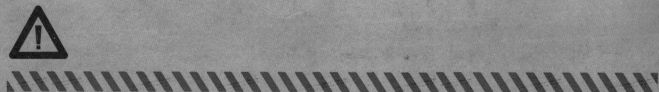

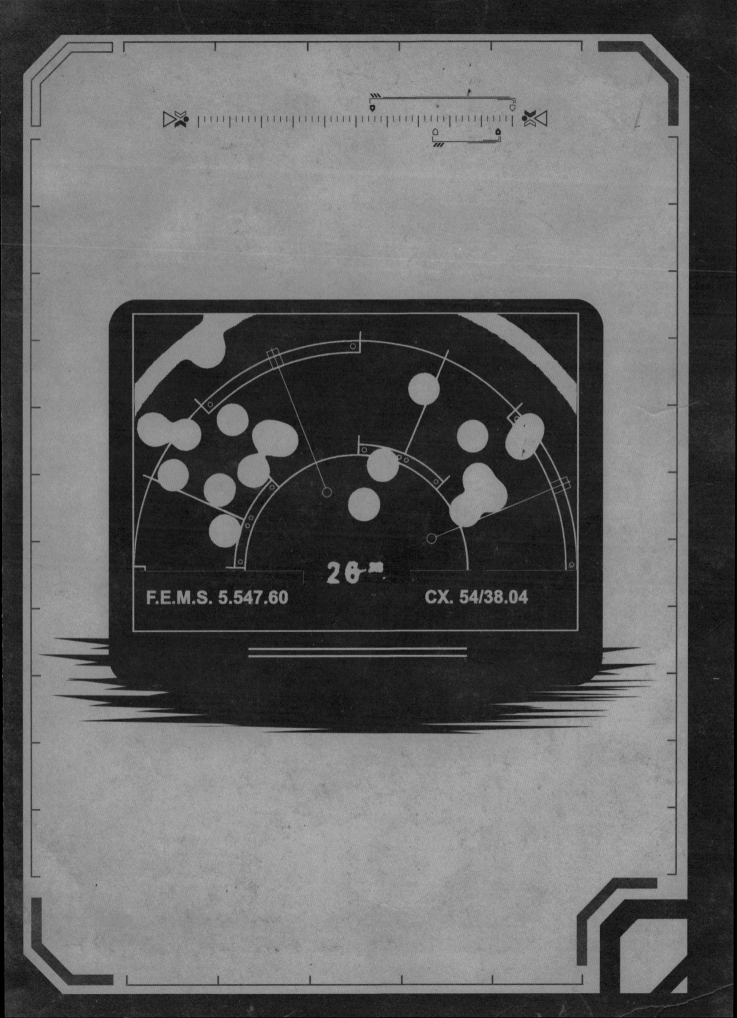

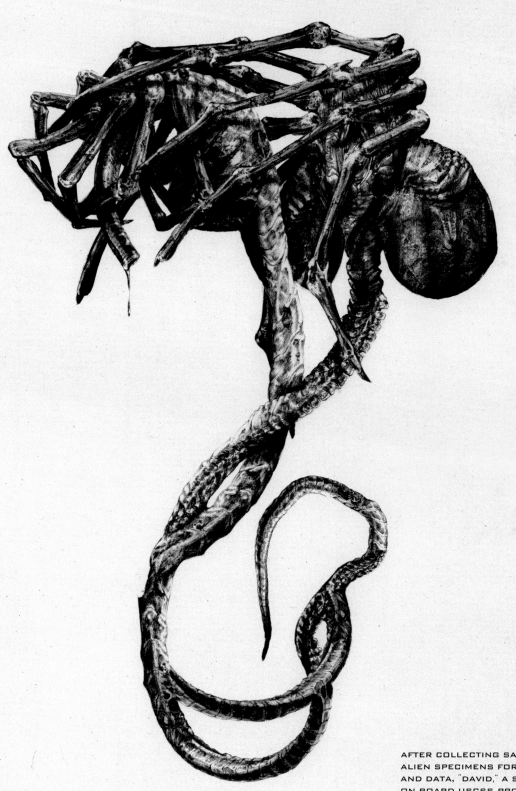

AFTER COLLECTING SAMPLES OF
ALIEN SPECIMENS FOR RESEARCH
AND DATA, "DAVID," A SYNTHETIC
ON BOARD USCSS *PROMETHEUS*
IN 2089 RECORDED HIS NOTES
AND SKETCHES.

MISSION DETAILS

Following the destruction of the USCSS *Nostromo* and her escape in its lifeboat the *Narcissus*, Ellen Ripley drifted in hypersleep for 57 years before being rescued and taken to Earth's orbiting Gateway Station.

Returning to civilian life following her debriefing, she was persuaded to return to LV-426 with a contingent of Colonial Marines when contact with the Hadley's Hope colony was lost in circumstances suggesting a Xenomorph incident.

Ripley, Second Battalion Bravo Team (including "Bishop," a synthetic) and Weyland-Yutani representative Carter Burke traveled back to the exo-moon aboard the USCSS *Sulaco*, and onward to the surface by drop-ship, where they found the colony had been overrun and turned into a Xenomorph hive dominated by a nesting Queen. Of the colonists, only one survivor was found: the juvenile Rebecca Jorden.

Creative attempts by Burke to procure Xenomorph specimens for Company study were unsuccessful, and a drop-ship crash caused a critical malfunction of the colony's power plant and the danger of an imminent, colossal thermonuclear explosion. This, coupled with aggressive defense of the nest by multiple Xenomorphs

and their surprisingly nimble Queen, necessitated swift evacuation of the exo-moon, and prompted the decision to cleanse the Xenomorph population from space by means of a nuclear strike.

Burke, and the entire U.S.C.M. platoon—with the exception of Corporal Dwayne Hicks—were all casualties of ferocious Xenomorph attacks. The Bishop synthetic was able to summon the *Sulaco*'s secondary drop-ship to facilitate the survivors' escape, which was successfully achieved, despite the unwitting transport of the Queen on the drop-ship's landing gear. Discovered once back aboard the *Sulaco*, the Queen was ejected by Ripley into open space via one of the *Sulaco*'s airlocks. The Bishop synthetic sustained near catastrophic damage during the fracas.

Following the requisite checks that all threats had been eradicated—which subsequently proved to have been inadequately carried out—Ripley, Jorden, the injured Hicks, and the damaged Bishop once again entered hypersleep for the return journey to Gateway.

BELOW LEFT: CREW'S TRAVEL TO LV-426 WAS DISTURBED DURING HYPERSLEEP IN CAPSULES.

ABOVE AND BELOW: DESPITE ITS INHOSPITABLE ATMOSPHERE, LV-426 WAS HOME TO A COLONY.

KEY PERSONNEL

LIEUTENANT ELLEN RIPLEY

Lone survivor of the USCSS *Nostromo*. Latterly civilian liaison to the U.S.M.C., promoted to rank for the purpose of the USCSS *Sulaco*'s mission.

CARTER BURKE

Junior executive with the Weyland-Yutani Corporation, and Special Projects Director for its Space Corps Special Services division. His strategy for capturing Xenomorph specimens on LV-426 was laudably ambitious but ultimately foolhardy.

REBECCA JORDEN

Lone survivor of the Hadley's Hope "shake and bake" terraforming colony. Also known by the familiar diminutive "Newt."

CORPORAL DWAYNE HICKS

Sole surviving marine following the Hadley's Hope debacle. Initially thought to have died in stasis aboard the *Sulaco*, but this may have been Company misinformation. Unconfirmed sightings place him subsequently on the USS *Legato*, the USS *Sephora*, and on Fiorina 161.

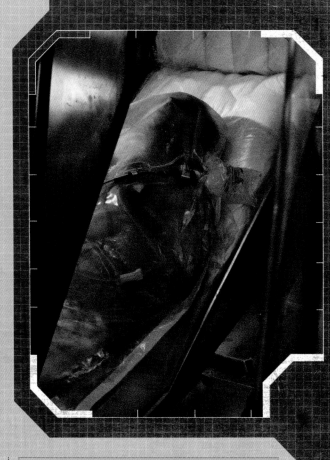

PRIVATE WILLIAM HUDSON

Veteran of several "bug hunts," although not committed to indefinite life in the U.S.M.C. Hudson considered himself to be serving time in pursuit of a sizable pension. His ten-year commission was mere weeks from completion when he was deployed to LV-426.

PRIVATE JENETTE VASQUEZ

Smartgun operator who enlisted in the U.S.M.C. after a troubled early life. Justifiably reputed to have issues with authority, she was nevertheless a capable Marine, surviving longer than most of the rest of her platoon during the Hadley's Hope encounter. Believed to have committed suicide rather than be captured for Xenomorph gestation.

ABOVE: THE M577 ARMORED PERSONNEL CARRIED IS STANDARD MARINE ISSUE.

LEFT: HYPERSLEEP CAPSULES CAN BE DANGEROUS IF NOT ADEQUATELY SEALED.

EXECUTIVE OFFICER ÙBISHOPI

Model 341-B synthetic technician: considerably advanced from the "Ash" model, and programmed with Asimov's *Three Laws of Robotics*, forbidding him to harm, or allow to come to harm, any human being. Designed by and modelled after Weyland-Yutani's senior robotics scientist Michael Bishop.

PRIVATE TREVOR WIERZBOWSKI

Little is officially recorded of the maverick commonly known as "Ski," or "Wierz-Man." Apparently one of the earliest casualties of Second Battalion Bravo Team at Hadley's Hope, rumors persist of his survival. Uncorroborated reports suggest a subsequent career running covert black-ops for Weyland-Yutani.

USCSS SULACO

The USCSS *Sulaco* was a Weyland-Yutani constructed, Conestoga-class transport ship. A typical twenty-second Century workhorse design, it had been much modified, added to, and jury-rigged by the time of the LV-426 U.S.M.C. mission in 2179. One observer called it "a floating scrap pile."

As was standard for the Conestoga class, the *Sulaco* was approximately 1,150 feet long with a mass approaching 86,000 tons. Its engines were powered by a Tachyon shunt hyperdrive, and it had, prior to 2179, carried crews of up to 90, although its automated systems, uploaded to a 28-terabyte mainframe, were such that the ship could function adequately with a significantly smaller crew contingent. Passenger manifests of up to 2,000 troops were not unusual, with the ship therefore capable of carrying that number of hypersleep pods and appropriate medical facilities if hanger space was utilized.

Aside from troop transport, the *Sulaco* and its fleet siblings were designed as carriers for the rapid deployment of drop-ships and other smaller vehicles. While they were not specifically intended for combat, they were nevertheless also battle-ready, with appropriate outer armor and a stock of weapons. The latter included railguns, 800-megavolt particle beams, orbital mines, infrared lasers, antisatellite missiles, and nukes.

Reports of the *Sulaco*'s demise are contradictory. Different sources claim its destruction as the result of Xenomorph infestation or collateral damage from the explosion of the USS *Sephora*. Its final location is also hard to pinpoint, but it is generally agreed to have been somewhere between LV-426 and Fiorina 161.

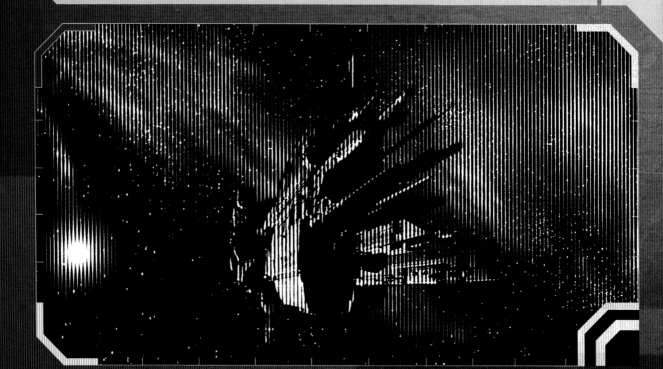

UD-4L "CHEYENNE" UTILITY DROP-SHIP

AIR INTAKES (PORT AND STARBOARD)

TAIL FIN

ROCKET PODS (BANSHEE 70)

25MM GATLING GUN

HELLBOUND MISSILES

LEFT: USS *SULACO* FLYOVER.

BELOW: UD-4L UTILITY DROP-SHIPS FERRY SUPPLIES, TROOPS, AND CIVILIANS.

ALIEN ANATOMY:
GROWTH AND LIFE EXPECTANCY

The transformation of the Chestburster into the fully grown Xenomorph seems to happen with incredible—some might claim improbable—speed. The Drone responsible for the *Nostromo* incident, for example, managed to almost double its initial size within a matter of hours. This, it must be made absolutely clear, was in a hostile environment where nourishment was not available from the carcass of its host; the creature achieved its impressive stature by simple scavenging. Some Company scientists theorize that the Xenomorph can even break down solid structures, such as rock and metal, with its acid secretions, providing itself with growth-fueling nutrients when no obvious sustenance is available. As with so much regarding these creatures, this hypothesis remains unproven.

A Xenomorph left to mature in ideal circumstances would, we must conclude, reach full maturity *even faster* than the *Nostromo* Drone. Scientists aboard the USCM *Auriga* reported that their captive Xenomorphs' growth rates could be observed with the naked eye.

Some of the earliest reports currently known to exist suggest a very short life-span, perhaps only a matter of days, like that of a mayfly. This would fit with its accelerated growth cycle. Preliminary studies suggested this could also have been the reason for the *Nostromo* Drone's apparently slowing down as its battle with Ellen Ripley became more and more protracted.

Other evidence, however, has suggested that the Xenomorph can easily outlive a human being and is capable of long periods of hibernation. The speed in which the species can destroy and exhaust an environment (or entire planet) of its life would seem to make this probable, allowing the Xenomorph to become dormant while re-population occurs. Eggs, as described elsewhere in this manual, are known to be able to survive for centuries.

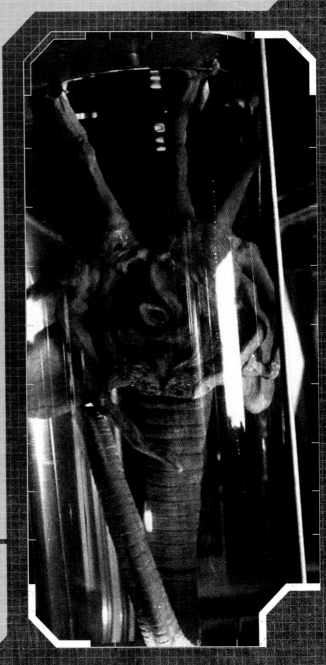

M240 INCINERATOR UNIT

A powerful liquid-fueled flamethrower with an effective range of 90 feet (which can be increased via creative deployment, such as arcing the flame upward or ricocheting from surfaces). Ultra-thickened Napthal fuel is stored under pressure either in a canister attached to the weapon or sourced from an attached main supply (usually a backpack worn by the operator). The fuel is then ignited as it leaves the weapon's barrel by a gas burner at the nozzle. Fuel can also be sprayed at a target unlit. This allows for a short period in which the fuel begins to vaporize, causing a fireball effect on eventual ignition.

Highly effective at close quarters, the M240 should obviously not be used in areas where other volatile combustible elements are present.

The M240 has been used on at least one occasion in an ad-hoc lash-up with the M41A Pulse Rifle. Such a system is not recommended in official U.S.C.M.C. guidelines.

TOP AND RIGHT: AS LIEUTENANT RIPLEY DISCOVERED, FLAME IS ONE OF THE MOST EFFECTIVE DISPATCH METHOD FOR OVOMORPHS AND FULLY GROWN ALIENS ALIKE.

RIGHT BELOW: CHESTBURSTERS CAN BE NEGATED WITH FIRE.

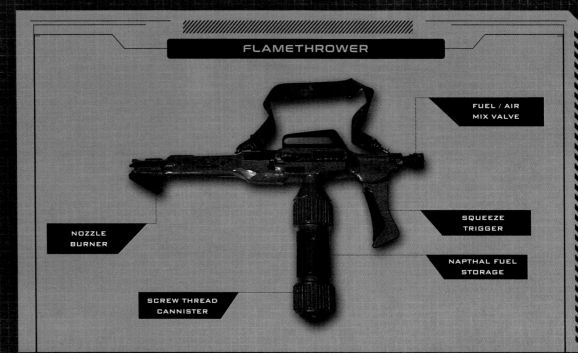

FLAMETHROWER

FUEL / AIR MIX VALVE

SQUEEZE TRIGGER

NAPTHAL FUEL STORAGE

NOZZLE BURNER

SCREW THREAD CANNISTER

MARINE BASIC TRAINING:
FIGHTING SKILLS

So-called "Bug Hunts" are only undertaken in rare circumstances. When an assessment deems that the risk level is acceptable, however, Marines may occasionally be sent to clear a hive or nest and eradicate a Xenomorph presence from an area entirely.

In such a case, by far the preferred tactic is to clear a scene of all civilian and military personnel, establish a sizable quarantine zone, and undertake reconnaissance with Drones and synthetics to establish methods of destroying the nest while dormant. (Note: Machines and synthetic life forms seem not to attract the Xenomorph's attention, being perceived neither as threats or potential hosts.)

Where circumstances dictate that Marines must enter a hive, the weaponry on hand is actually less important than the accuracy and effectiveness in which it's deployed. You may feel powerful and relatively safe strapped into an M56, but the power of your weapon is irrelevant if you're not hitting anything with it. Remain calm and do not fire in panic, because you risk hitting your fellow Marines as well as the enemy.

Keep in mind also that this will not be a traditional firefight. The enemy will not be firing back, but will be rushing you in waves of multiple targets with the intention of physically tearing you to pieces. The Xenomorph is not intimidated by weaponry of any kind, and while far from bulletproof, it can withstand multiple hits without slowing down.

Platoons are, of course, backed up by drop-ships, which may be called in for air strikes as and when such action is deemed necessary. As an absolutely last resort, the one sure-fire method of condemning a hive is to nuke it from space. This, of course, renders the site uninhabitable for decades afterward and runs the risk of extensive collateral damage. But if the worst comes to the worst, it's the only way to be sure.

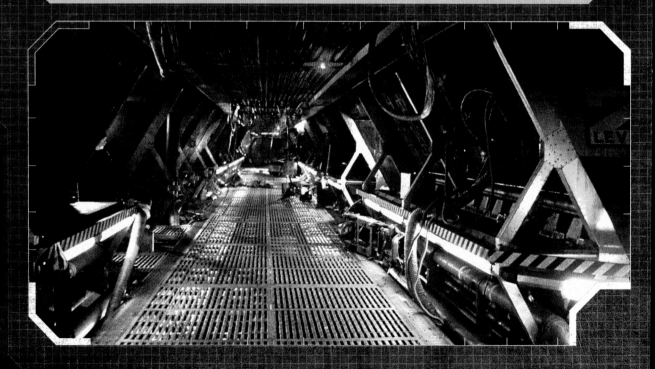

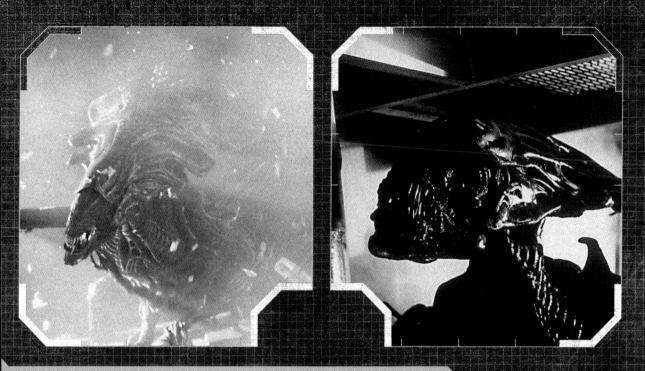

LEFT: SPACESHIP CORRIDORS ARE, UNFORTUNATELY, WHERE XENOMORPH
ENCOUNTERS TAKE PLACE; FAMILIARITY IS ESSENTIAL.

ABOVE AND BELOW: EXAMPLES OF ALIEN TERMINATION.

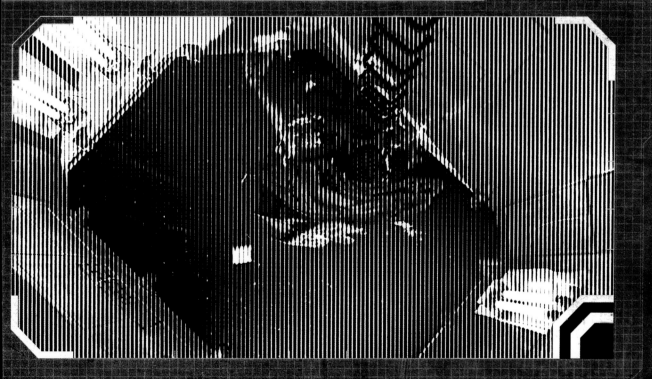

PERFECT ORGANISM: WARRIOR

By far the most common caste of Xenomorph you will probably encounter in the field is the Warrior. These are fully formed adults and can be differentiated from the largely similar Drones by their ridged skulls. They can grow to as much as 7 feet 6 inches tall, and when moving on all fours, their length, including tail, can be 15 feet long.

The Warrior is fast, vicious, strong, and extremely adaptable to environments and situations. Essentially bipedal when spawned from a human host, it can nevertheless travel equally efficiently on four legs, climb walls, and cling to ceilings. It can also negotiate small spaces, such as vents and ducts; jump great distances; and swim at speed, propelled with the aid of its 6-foot 6-inch-long bladed tail.

The Warrior's outer carapace is a tough, chitinous armor, and as with all variations of the Xenomorph, its blood is a highly pressurized and concentrated molecular acid that can eat through solid matter, including concrete and metal. This means that, while vulnerable to projectile weapons, they remain dangerous when injured; a bleeding Xenomorph is even more deadly than an undamaged one. When subject to extreme physical trauma, they have been observed to explode, showering their immediate vicinity with corrosive plasma. Needless to say, when this happens, you do not want to be near them.

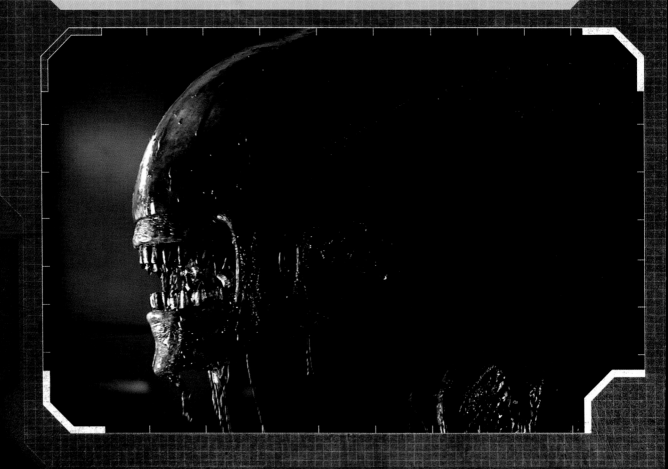

Body armor and protective clothing are to be worn at all times. They will not, ultimately, make you invincible to exposure, but they are better than nothing.

The Warriors' intelligence levels are debatable. On one hand, they have occasionally appeared capable of stealth tactics, on one occasion even appearing to deliberately cut a facility's power. On the other hand, they demonstrate more mindless, swarmlike behavior, attacking head on, en mass, even if it means a high casualty rate among their own numbers. These contradictory traits may be attributable to their telepathic connection to the Queen, who could theoretically be manipulating the warriors' behavior according to context.

FAR LEFT: IF YOU GET THIS CLOSE TO A WARRIOR, SURVIVAL WILL BE YOUR ONLY PRIORITY.

BELOW: EXAMPLES OF WARRIORS AND THEIR TERRIFYING STRENGTH AND ABILITY TO HARM HUMANS.

REMEMBER: WHERE THERE IS A WORKER, THERE WILL PROBABLY BE A HIVE AND A QUEEN— APPROACH WITH EXTREME CAUTION.

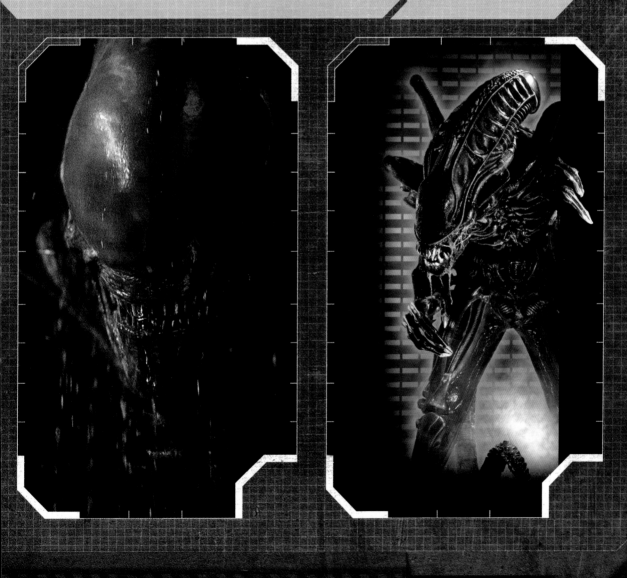

ALIEN ANATOMY: KNOW YOUR ENEMY
IMPLANTING

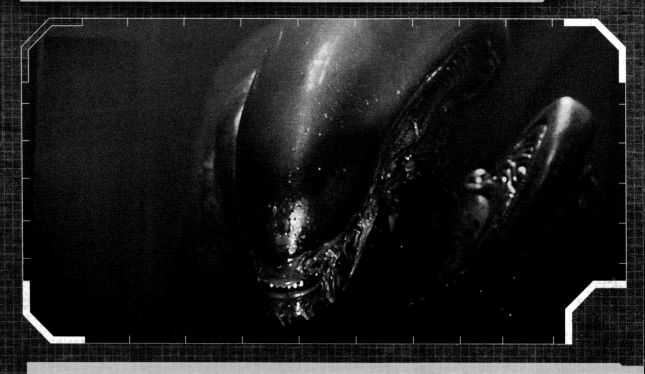

Rendering its victim comatose by secretion of a paralytic chemical agent, the Facehugger uses its proboscis to implant the nascent Chestburster into the victim's chest cavity via the esophagus.

While attached, the Facehugger breathes for its moribund host via the implantation proboscis. Intriguingly, this process appears to be unaffected by environment or species. The Facehugger seems able to adapt to whatever atmosphere its host requires.

The Facehugger detaches from its host and dies once the implantation/impregnation process is complete. Death of the host does not appear to affect gestation if a successful impregnation has already taken place. In a nest or hive setting, hosts are generally held captive, bound by the Xenomorph's distinctive secreted resin, in much the way that a spider will wrap a fly in its webbing. Outside of this setting, however, hosts have been observed to make a temporary recovery once the Facehugger has removed itself. This state of reprieve can last four hours or days. We do not yet understand why Xenomorph gestation times vary to this extent.

Different schools of thought exist on the nature of the Chestburster organism when first implanted. For many years, it was assumed to be a relatively simple embryo, growing to maturity as it fed on its host. More recently, however, a counter theory has emerged suggesting that the Facehugger in fact implants cells that behave similarly to cancers. In this scenario, the host's body would develop the Chestburster from its own genetic material.

Once it reaches the appropriate point in its gestation, the Chestburster begins to secrete enzymes that soften the internal chest cavity of the host. This facilitates its forceful bursting out through the host's sternum, resulting in massive physical trauma and the host's instant death. At this most vulnerable stage in its development, the juvenile Xenomorph will immediately seek a safe place in which to mature. If undisturbed—for example, in a nest environment—when it emerges, the juvenile will use the carcass of its host for nourishment.

A XENOMORPH IS
THE END RESULT
OF THE ENEMY
CREATION
LIFECYCLE:

1) ENGINEER

2) HUMAN

3) AI SYNTHETIC

4) XENOMORPH

MEMORIZE
EACH STAGE TO
UNDERSTAND
YOUR ENEMY'S
WEAKNESSES.

LEFT: CERTAIN XENOMORPHS
ARE CURIOUS ABOUT THEIR
PREY...

ABOVE: ... AND WILL APPROACH
FOR INSPECTION BEFORE
GOING FOR THE KILL.

BELOW: VIDEO SEQUENCE OF
AN IMPLANTED ALIEN BEING
EXTRACTED FROM ITS HOST.

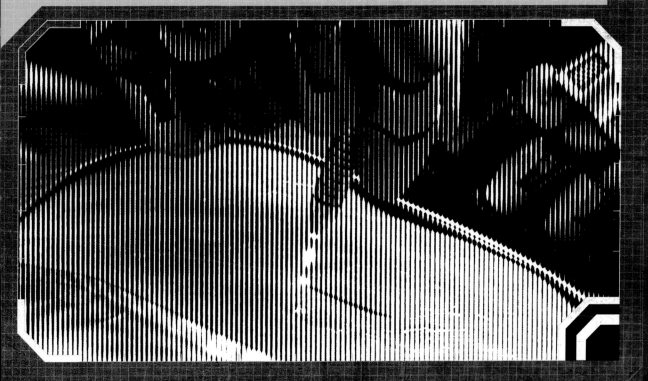

USS SULACO TRANSMISSIONS

TRANSMISSIONS FROM THE FIELD CAN PROVIDE VALUABLE INFORMATION ABOUT THE HISTORY AND ORIGINS OF THE ALIEN THREAT, AS WELL AS USEFUL CLUES ABOUT THE WORKINGS OF THE MARINE CORPS. THE FOLLOWING WERE ALL CAPTURED AROUND THE USS *SULACO* INTERACTION IN 2122

> YOU WERE OUT THERE FOR 57 YEARS. WHAT HAPPENED WAS, YOU HAD DRIFTED RIGHT THROUGH THE CORE SYSTEMS, AND IT'S REALLY JUST BLIND LUCK THAT A DEEP SALVAGE TEAM FOUND YOU WHEN THEY DID. IT'S ONE IN A THOUSAND, REALLY. I THINK YOU'RE DAMN LUCKY TO BE ALIVE, KIDDO. YOU COULD BE FLOATING OUT THERE FOREVER.
> —BURKE TO RIPLEY

> I DON'T KNOW WHICH SPECIES IS WORSE. YOU DON'T SEE THEM FUCKING EACH OTHER OVER FOR A GODDAMN PERCENTAGE.
> —RIPLEY

> DID IQS JUST DROP SHARPLY WHILE I WAS AWAY?
> —RIPLEY

> MY MOMMY ALWAYS SAID THERE WERE NO MONSTERS— NO REAL ONES—BUT THERE ARE.
> —NEWT

> **"** ALL RIGHT, SWEETHEARTS, WHAT ARE YOU WAITING FOR? BREAKFAST IN BED? ANOTHER GLORIOUS DAY IN THE CORPS! A DAY IN THE MARINE CORPS IS LIKE A DAY ON THE FARM. EVERY MEAL'S A BANQUET! EVERY PAYCHECK A FORTUNE! EVERY FORMATION A PARADE! I LOVE THE CORPS! **"**
> —SERGEANT APONE

> **"** IS THIS GONNA BE A STAND-UP FIGHT OR ANOTHER BUG HUNT? **"**
> —HUDSON

> **"** ALL WE KNOW IS THAT THERE'S STILL NO CONTACT WITH THE COLONY AND THAT A XENOMORPH MAY BE INVOLVED. **"**
> —GORMAN

> **"** I KNOW THIS IS AN EMOTIONAL MOMENT FOR ALL OF US, BUT LET'S NOT MAKE SNAP JUDGMENTS, PLEASE. THIS IS CLEARLY AN IMPORTANT SPECIES WE'RE DEALING WITH AND I DON'T THINK THAT ANYBODY HAS THE RIGHT TO ARBITRARILY EXTERMINATE THEM. **"**
> —BURKE

> **"** REMEMBER: SHORT, CONTROLLED BURSTS. **"**
> —HICKS

BEST OF THE BEST:
ELLEN RIPLEY: LAST SURVIVOR OF THE *NOSTROMO*

Perhaps surprisingly, the individual with the greatest repeated success at combating and defeating the Xenomorph is not a Marine, but a civilian (her essentially honorary Lieutenant status notwithstanding). While her repeated insistence on destroying the alien, instead of assisting in its capture for study and development, put her at odds with the Weyland-Yutani agenda, Ellen Ripley's Xenomorph encounters can nevertheless teach us a great deal about the importance of ingenuity, tenacity,and guerrilla tactics in fighting the creature—when fighting is the only option.

Aboard the USCSS *Nostromo*, Ripley attempted to follow correct protocols in refusing to allow unidentified specimens to be brought aboard ship—although these protocols were overridden by other crew members, whether wittingly or unwittingly working to Company orders. When control of the situation was lost and the crew suffered multiple casualties, Ripley's attempted to initiate self-destruct and destroy the alien along with the *Nostromo* as she escaped in the *Narcissus* lifeboat. When the alien was revealed to be aboard the *Narcissus* with her, she donned an IRC Mk.50 compression suit to survive the vacuum while ejecting the alien from an airlock. Ripley also used a grappling hook during the ensuing scuffle, and was finally able to eject the alien from the ship completely by activating the engine to which it still clung.

Airlock ejection also proved effective in defeating the Xenomorph Queen during the *Sulaco* incident. In this case, Ripley managed to survive the vacuum of space with no protection. As a tactic, opening an airlock when not wearing a compression suit should be considered an absolutely final resort—and potentially suicidal. Earlier in the protracted battle, Ripley had found a Caterpillar P-5000 Work Loader to be useful as both weapon and armor; and had found the Ovopods to be particularly susceptible to a flamethrower. She also discovered the useful intelligence that the Xenomorph—whether Queen or Drone—will not attack if doing so places eggs (and by extension Xenomorph juveniles) under threat.

Subsequently, on Fiorina 161, the successful tactic proved to be bait and trap, Ripley and her improvised unit lured the alien Runner into a foundry molding facility and doused it with molten lead. When the creature emerged, having survived this initial salvo, Ripley activated a sprinkler system. The action of the cold water on the alien's superheated exoskeleton caused the creature to explode. Because she had been gestating a Xenomorph Queen in her chest cavity throughout the events on the prison moon, Ripley's final action was to throw herself into the foundry's furnace, killing both herself and the alien.

Reports of Ripley's revival aboard the *Auriga* are muddled; this individual was a clone, its DNA melded with that of the Xenomorph. Her actions cannot exactly be attributed as those of Ellen Ripley. However, destruction of the "Newborn" creature was effected.

RIGHT: RIPLEY DEALS WITH A CLUSTER OF OVOMORPHS IN AN EFFECTIVE MANNER.

BELOW: RIPLEY'S KNOWLEDGE OF XENOMORPHS SURPASSES THAT OF ANY OTHER HUMAN.

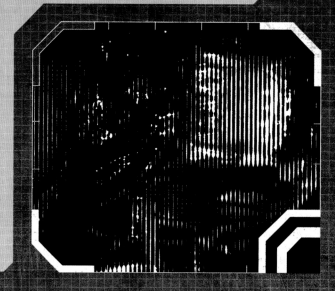

MISSION DETAILS

With Ripley, Hicks, and Jorden in hypersleep and the damaged Bishop synthetic offline, the *Sulaco*'s autopilot systems were engaged to return the ship to Gateway Station, orbiting Earth. Unbeknownst to the survivors, however, at least two Facehuggers were still loose aboard the ship.

One of the creatures injured itself in attempting to access Jorden's cryo-pod, its acid blood disrupting some core *Sulaco* systems, leading the ship to eject its occupants. The escape vehicle subsequently crash-landed on the penal colony and foundry facility Fiorina "Fury" 161, approximately 19.5 light-years from its intended destination.

Neither Jorden or Hicks survived the crash, and Ripley, following rescue and examination by the facility's medical officer Clemens, was found to have been impregnated by the Facehugger with an alien Queen. Contradictory reports also indicate that a second Facehugger escaped the crash and quickly impregnated either a dog or an ox on the facility's outskirts, leading to the swift birth of a quadrupedal Runner alien. Loose in the facility, the Runner was able to kill several inmates and staff before counter measures were attempted.

An initial plan to trap the alien in the facility's nuclear waste tank was initially successful—although casualties were incurred when walls coated with Quinitricetyline were ignited prematurely. The creature was, however, deliberately freed again by the prisoner Golic, suffering a religious mania that led him to believe the Xenomorph was a "dragon" of divine purpose.

Regrouping, Ripley and the inmates then formed a new plan to bait the alien into the foundry's molds and furnaces. Once there, the creature was first doused in molten lead and then in cold water. The rapid fluctuations in temperature extremes causing its carapace to expand, contract, crack, and ultimately shatter.

Weyland-Yutani representatives arrived at the facility too late to prevent the creature's destruction, or to capture the Queen gestating within Ripley. Ripley's deliberate fall into the furnace killed both her and the Chestburster within her. The prison's sole survivor, Morse, was evacuated, and the facility itself shut down.

FURY 161 CLASS C PRISON UNIT IRIS — 12037154
REPORT EEV UNIT 2650 CRASH
ONE SURVIVOR — LT.RIPLEY — B5156170
DEAD CPL.HICKS L55321
DEAD UNIDENTIFIED FEMALE APRX. 10 YRS OLD
REQUEST EMERG.EVAC SOONEST POSSIBLE —
AWAIT RESPONSE — SUPT.ANDREWS M51021

LEFT: THE INMATES DIAGNOSED WITH DOUBLE
Y CHROMOSOME SYNDROME, EXPERIENCED
TWO FACEHUGGERS AFTER THE USCSS *SULACO*
EJECTED ITS ESCAPE SHIP.

TOP RIGHT: CHESTBURSTERS CAN USE LIVE
STEER AS HOSTS. AFTER BIRTH, THEY USUALLY
SPRINT OFF, AND DEMONSTRATE CAT-LIKE
AGILITY.

RIGHT: THE MINERAL OIL REFINERY MACHINE
WORKED BY INMATES ON THE OUTER VEIL
COLONY FIORINA "FURY" 161, LOCATED IN THE
NERIOD SECTOR.

BELOW: A DISSECTION OF THE HOST CAN
PROVIDE DETAILS ON THE ENEMY'S NEW FORM.

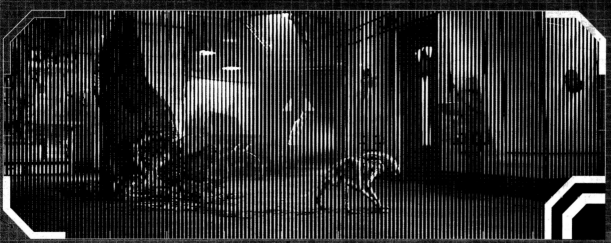

KEY PERSONNEL

ELLEN RIPLEY

Last survivor of the *Nostromo* and the *Sulaco*.

LEONARD DILLON

Fiorina "Fury" 161 Correctional Unit inmate, incarcerated for murder and rape. Self-styled leader of an apocalyptic religion that spread among the prisoners.

JONATHAN CLEMENS

Former "Fury" inmate and subsequent Weyland-Yutani employee. Convicted of manslaughter, having caused several deaths due to negligence as a result of substance addiction. Stayed on after his sentence as the facility's medical officer.

HAROLD ANDREWS

Warden of the "Fury" facility, in the employ of Weyland-Yutani. Respected for his insistence on "rumor control," which he countered with "the facts." Initial refusal to take the Xemomorph threat seriously arguably exacerbated its effects.

FRANCIS AARON

Veteran of several "bug hunts," although not committed to indefinite life in the U.S.M.C. Hudson considered himself to be serving time in pursuit of a sizable pension. His ten-year commission was mere weeks from completion when he was deployed to LV-426.

WALTER GOLIC

"Fury" inmate serving an indefinite sentence for multiple murders, dismemberment, and arson. One of the facility's most disturbed individuals. Believed the Xenomorph to be a "dragon" of divine origin, and was responsible for its release after its initial capture.

MICHAEL BISHOP

Weyland-Yutani roboticist and inventor of the "Bishop" synthetic line. Arrived on Fiorina 161 as a Company representative, too late to facilitate the live capture of the loose Runner or the nascent Queen within Ripley.

LEFT: STASIS CARRIES THE RISK OF SIDE EFFECTS, INCLUDING EXHAUSTION AND DIZZINESS.

TOP RIGHT: EXPOSED XENOMORPH RIB CAGES ARE YOUR FIRST POINT OF ATTACK.

BOTTOM RIGHT: THE DEATH OF MICHAEL BISHOP IS CLASSIFIED INFORMATION. NOT FOR PUBLIC DISCLOSURE.

RESTRICTED CASE FILE:
FIORINA "FURY" 161

Fiorina 161, colloquially known as "Fury," is a barren planet in the Neroid Sector, 19.5 light-years from Earth. Inhospitable due to large areas of both desert and ocean, high winds, and extremes of temperature, it nevertheless has an atmosphere breathable by humans, and was utilized in the twenty-second century for industrial projects.

Following exhaustion of Fury's natural resources by mining operations, the most notable among its facilities were its lead smelting plant and its Class C Work Correctional Unit for maximum security inmates. Both were owned by the Weyland-Yutani corporation. The latter at one point in its history housed 5,000 Double-Y chromosome prisoners, until a change in political climate saw it largely closed down.

A skeleton contingent of 22 inmates, all of whom had adopted an ad-hoc, apocalyptic religious system, opted at this point to stay behind with a small supervisory staff to maintain the lead works and practice their faith in isolation. All structures were finally officially closed and abandoned following the Xenomorph incident in 2179.

RIGHT: RUNNERS, OR DOG ALIENS, MOVE DIFFERENTLY TO OTHER XENOMORPHS AND SPIT ACID FROM THEIR MOUTHS. BEWARE OF THEIR SPEED AND AGILITY.

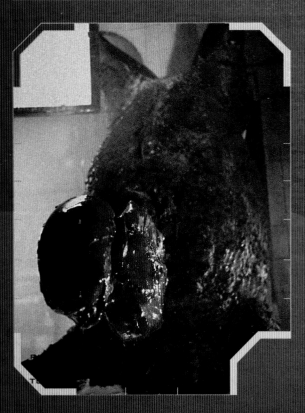

EEV

The Type 337 Emergency Escape Vehicle (EEV) was the standard lifeboat for ships in the *Sulaco*'s class during the twenty-second century. Measuring just over 43 feet long, it was capable of carrying five passengers; it was fully automated and integrated with its mothership's systems, needing no flight crew (although the pods could be ejected manually). During flight, the Type 337 was typically on 30-second standby.

As part of its core suite of systems, the Type 337 supported cryo-tube ejections, meaning that crew members in hypersleep did not need to be revived during an emergency. Hibernating crew members could be disconnected from the mothership's mainframe, and auto loaded into the lifeboat via transport shafts, where they were then reconnected to the EEV's own life-support systems. If no abort command was received during the process, the Type 337 detached itself from the docking ring holding it to the mothership in a series of stages, and was propelled outwards by the mothership's own atmosphere. The time taken to achieve this entire process was usually no more than 45 seconds.

An independently operating EEV would then scan nearby space and head for the nearest navigational beacon, while at the same time broadcasting its own emergency distress signal.

ABOVE: A WEYLAND-YUTANI COMMANDO TEAM WAS DEPLOYED TO CLOSE THE SITUATION.

BELOW AND LEFT: OIL REFINERY MACHINERY ON FIORINA "FURY" 161.

WEAPONRY: TOOLS OF YOUR TRADE

M56 SMARTGUN

Capable of firing 1,200 rounds per minute, the M56A2 Smart Gun is every Marine's best friend. First rolled out in 2172, this fully automatic, general-purpose machine gun has a medium to high strike accuracy. The weapon requires no setup or positioning before opening fire; just point and shoot. In the right Marine's hands, this is the only weapon required to make a tight spot loose. U.S.C.M. doctrine dictates that at least one gunner Marine per Gun Team carries the M56 Smartgun on all missions, providing heavy fire support for the rest of the squad armed only with their M41As.

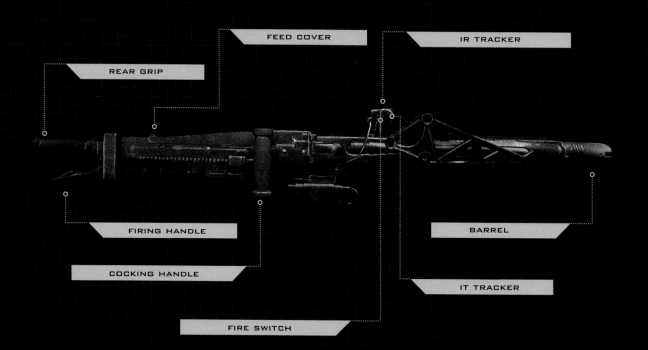

FEED COVER

IR TRACKER

REAR GRIP

FIRING HANDLE

BARREL

COCKING HANDLE

IT TRACKER

FIRE SWITCH

G2 ELECTROSHOCK GRENADE

Marines have nicknamed this powerful grenade the "Sonic Electronic Bouncing Betty," or "Ball Breaker," due to its detonation height and its destructive ability to a threat's central nervous system. Armed with a timer setting, ranging from three seconds to three minutes, the shock emitted from this bouncing mine grenade delivers electric current large enough to stun groups of advancing enemies and instantaneously paralyze for up to 30 minutes. Each Marine is armed with only two G2s, so deploy wisely.

M18A1 CLAYMORE MINE

The Claymore has a fatal strike range of 50 yards. Detonated by remote control, using a firing trigger wired into the mine, or trip-wire device, the M18A1 releases a rapid shotgun burst of steel balls within a 60-degree arc, facing forward from the mine. An effective weapon used primarily in tactical strategies, such as enemy ambush and anti-infiltration against advancing enemy combatants, the M18A1 has the words "FRONT TOWARD ENEMY" embossed on the front. Vital reading for all Marines.

UA 571-C AUTOMATED SENTRY GUN

A tripod-mounted fully-automated 360 degree perimeter defense system capable of firing 1,100 bursts per minute from its M30 Autocannon, the UA 571-C Automated Sentry Gun can be assembled in under three minutes and weighs less than 45 pounds. Affectionately nicknamed "Robot Sentry" by U.S.C. Marines, the weapon comes equipped with three operating modes: Auto-Remote, Manual Override, and Semi-Automatic.

MARINE BASIC TRAINING: HOW TO KILL MORE ALIENS

Taking the fight to the Xenomorph is rarely possible, or indeed, advisable, at ground level. In practice, Marines have almost exclusively found themselves in positions where a strong defense is a necessity. This need not be seen as a weak position.

A position of defense is not always the result of being taken by surprise. A good defense buys time and helps develop the conditions for effective offensive operations, such as air strikes from dropships. It may also be key to retaining an important facility or piece of terrain from Xenomorph infestation. It can even be effective in concentrating the Xenomorph's attention on a specific area, leaving another relatively unguarded. The latter should be considered only as an extreme measure. This is because deliberately attracting Xenomorphs to a position rarely ends well for those fighting against them. Marines should not be encouraged to use each other as bait, and individuals

BELOW: SOLDIER XENOMORPHS CAN ENDURE INTENSE HEAT AND ARE PRONE TO SNEAK ATTACKS. WATCH ALL QUADRANTS.

should not be tempted to martyr themselves, even if they believe it to be for the good of the unit.

Effective preparation of a defensive position allows a Marine to turn the tables to his advantage; the terrain should be far more familiar to you than to the Xenomorph by the time the Xenomorph reaches your position and attacks. Appropriate setup of the UA571-C Remote Automated Sentry System (see Weapons section), for example, is essential for thinning Xenomorph numbers during a swarm attack both in open and confined spaces.

In the latter scenario, pay attention to sealing doors and other ingresses; welding (as opposed to barricading) is the fail-safe. Do not be complacent. Be aware of vents, shafts, tunnels, and crawl spaces: the Xenomorph is adaptable and flexible. Motion trackers should be equipped at all times as an early alert to Xenomorph activity behind walls, above ceilings, and below floors.

ABOVE: WARRIOR XENOMORPHS CAN OPEN DOORS.
RIGHT: ALWAYS DOUBLE CHECK A XENOMORPH IS DEAD.

PERFECT ORGANISM:
WORKER

The most basic adult form of the Xenomorph, the Worker (or "Drone") differs little from the Warrior caste, but is less developed. The principal characteristic separating the two discrete stages is the domelike head carapace, which is replaced with the more usual ridged skull as the creature ages. The reason for this is unclear, but it is possible that the dome keeps the creature separate from the hive mind of its elders. The Drone appears to be smarter than the Warrior and capable of existing independently from the Queen. The domeless Warriors seem to not have this autonomy.

Marines should not infer diminished threat from the Drone's immaturity. A single drone was responsible for the loss of the *Nostromo* and its crew.

The common trait shared by all adult Xenomorphs—and some juveniles in Chestburster form—is the unique inner mouth. This secondary set of jaws and teeth is housed within the Xenomorph's primary outer jaw at the end of a prehensile tongue. This proboscis can be forcefully ejected and retracted from the outer jaw in a pistonlike motion. The main function of the inner jaw seems to be that of attack, and in close quarters it is a devastatingly effective weapon.

The Xenomorph's usual method of deploying the "tongue" is to grip the head of a victim in its outer jaws and use the inner mechanism to punch a hole through the victim's cranium.

Weyland-Yutani scientists have developed a theory that the inner jaw could have a secondary function. Because the Xenomorph is to all intents and purposes blind, the tongue may possibly incorporate one of the sensory apparatus with which the creature perceives its environment.

LEFT: DRONE XENOMORPHS' INTRICATE SKELETAL CASINGS DISPLAY THEIR WEAKNESS.

BELOW LEFT: IF A DRONE SEEMS FLAME RESISTANT, TRY THE "WET-SHOT" TECHNIQUE.

TOP: WORKER XENOMORPH ARE THE LOWEST FORM OF THAT SPECIES. GIVE THEM HELL.

BELOW RIGHT: DRONE'S LARGE SMUG JAWS ARE MADE TO BE BROKEN.

DRONE / CLONED XENOMORPH

THE EXTRAORDINARY POWER AND EFFECTIVENESS OF THE
DRONE WAS DEMONSTRATED ON BOARD THE USCSS *NOSTROMO*,
WHERE THE MAJORITY OF HUMAN LIFE WAS EXTINGUISHED BY
A SINGLE CREATURE. WORKERS, WHICH CAN BE INCUBATED IN
HUMAN HOSTS, SOON OUTGROW THEIR HOSTS IN HEIGHT AND
STRENGTH. IT IS WIDELY BELIEVED THAT ADULT DRONES EVOLVE
INTO WARRIORS (SEE OTHER PAGES IN THIS MANUAL).

BASICS

HEIGHT: About 8 feet (total length including tail is 14 feet or more)
WEIGHT: About 350 pounds
SKIN COLOR: Black-gray
VARIANTS: Scout, Stalker, Worker

HEAD

Head carapace—smoothest of any Xenomorph.
As the Drone develops into a Warrior, this changes, developing ridges.

JAW / MOUTH

Bite strength in excess of 6,000psi.

INNER TOOTHED MANDIBULAR SET

Can extend more than 18 inches from the mouth,
and used to eliminate enemies if hands, feet,
tail, and outer jaw are unavailable.

ACIDIC SALIVA

The Drone is capable of spitting
at enemies, giving significant
range advantage.

ALIEN ANATOMY: KNOW YOUR ENEMY
PREFERRED HOSTS

Our knowledge of the Xenomorph and its life cycle comes form our observation of its interaction with our own species. We cannot know the efficiency of its interaction with other alien life-forms as yet unencountered by humankind. However, its is clear that the Xenomorph is hugely adaptable, capable of gestating within mammals other than humans, and arguably within the beings known as the Engineers.

One of the most fascinating aspects of the Xenomorph's life cycle is the way in which its initial host dictates its final form. As such, a Xenomorph gestated within a human or otherwise bipedal host will emerge as an essentially two-legged creature (the Warrior or Drone). But a Xenomorph that reaches its Chestburster form within a four-legged creature (say, for example, a dog or an ox) will develop into an adult Xenomorph quadruped, or "Runner."

As their names suggests, Runners are typically faster than their counterpart castes. They are also slightly weaker—although hardly less fearsome, able to spit acid and using their tails as weapons more than other castes—and have been witnessed attempting to outrun threats instead of facing them head on. They have the domed head of the Drone instead of the ridged skull of the Warrior, and there are some reports that they appear less intelligent than either. This possibly indicates that a Xenomorph derives mental capacity from its host as well as physical form.

The lone Xenomorph responsible for the incident on Fiorina 161 was a Runner.

As hosts, humans are apparently superior to other Earth-based mammals as vehicles for gestation in that they have a particularly appropriate chest cavity in which

the Xenomorph can be lodged; a bipedal stature that seems to suit the creature; and a high level of intelligence that also seems on some level to be inherited by the developing parasite. Aside from the controversial matter of the Engineer, the only other reports of Xenomorphs hatching from other alien life-forms are with similarly intelligent, bipedal species. These accounts are, however, uncorroborated and must be considered apocryphal.

LEFT: XENOMORPHS HAVE A LARGE CEREBRAL CAPACITY AND WILL NOT STOP HUNTING. YOU'RE ONLY CHOICE IS TO BEAT THEM TO IT.

ABOVE AND RIGHT: XENOMORPHS CAN GESTATE IN ANY LARGE LIVING CREATURE. A XENOMORPH THAT GESTATES IN A HUMAN WILL TAKE ON ELEMENTS OF ITS PHYSICAL ATTRIBUTES.

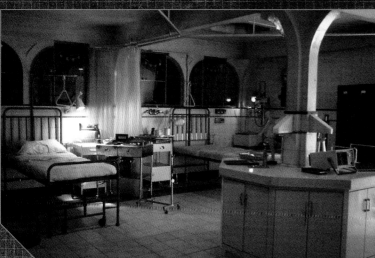

"FURY" 161

THE MEDICAL LAB ON FIORINA 161, WHERE LIEUTENANT RIPLEY AWOKE AS THE SOLE SURVIVOR OF USCSS *SULACO*. THE DOCTOR PERFORMED AN AUTOPSY ON NEWT IN THE LAB, ON THE INSISTENCE OF RIPLEY, WHO BELIEVED NEWT TO BE CARRYING AN ALIEN EMBRYO.

USCSS SULACO TRANSMISSIONS

TRANSMISSIONS FROM THE FIELD CAN PROVIDE VALUABLE INFORMATION ABOUT THE HISTORY AND ORIGINS OF THE ALIEN THREAT, AS WELL AS USEFUL CLUES ABOUT THE WORKINGS OF THE MARINE CORPS. THE FOLLOWING WERE ALL CAPTURED FROM FIORINA 161 IN 2179

> WHEN THEY FIRST HEARD ABOUT THIS THING, IT WAS 'CREW EXPENDABLE.' THE NEXT TIME THEY SENT IN MARINES—THEY WERE EXPENDABLE, TOO. WHAT MAKES YOU THINK THEY'RE GONNA CARE ABOUT A BUNCH OF LIFERS WHO FOUND GOD AT THE ASS-END OF SPACE? YOU REALLY THINK THEY'RE GONNA LET YOU INTERFERE WITH THEIR PLANS FOR THIS THING? THEY THINK WE'RE CRUD. AND THEY DON'T GIVE A FUCK ABOUT ONE FRIEND OF YOURS THAT'S DIED. NOT ONE.
>
> —RIPLEY

> LET ME SEE IF I HAVE THIS CORRECT, LIEUTENANT—IT'S AN 8-FOOT CREATURE OF SOME KIND WITH ACID FOR BLOOD, AND IT ARRIVED ON YOUR SPACESHIP. IT KILLS ON SIGHT, AND IS GENERALLY UNPLEASANT. QUITE A STORY...
>
> —ANDREWS

> YOU'VE BEEN IN MY LIFE SO LONG, I CAN'T REMEMBER ANYTHING ELSE.
>
> —RIPLEY

" YOU'RE ALL GONNA DIE. THE ONLY QUESTION IS HOW YOU
CHECK OUT. DO YOU WANT IT ON YOUR FEET? OR ON YOUR
FUCKIN' KNEES... BEGGING? I AIN'T MUCH FOR BEGGING!
NOBODY EVER GAVE ME NOTHING! SO I SAY FUCK THAT THING!
LET'S FIGHT IT! "
—DILLON

" GIVEN THE NATURE OF OUR INDIGENOUS POPULATION,
I WOULD SUGGEST CLOTHES. NONE OF THEM HAVE SEEN
A WOMAN IN YEARS. "
—CLEMENS

" WE HAVE SOME CARVING KNIVES IN THE ABATTOIR, A FEW
MORE IN THE MESS HALL. SOME FIRE AXES SCATTERED ABOUT
THE PLACE – NOTHING TERRIBLY FORMIDABLE. "
—ANDREWS

" I DON'T LIKE LOSIN' A FIGHT. NOT TO NOBODY, NOT TO NOTHIN'.
THAT DAMN THING OUT THERE'S ALREADY KILLED HALF MY MEN,
GOT THE OTHER HALF SCARED SHITLESS. AS LONG AS IT'S
ALIVE, SISTER, YOU'RE NOT GONNA SAVE ANY UNIVERSE. "
—DILLON

2379CE
USM AURIGA

MISSION DETAILS

Two centuries after the events on Fiorina 161, scientists aboard the United Systems Military vessel *Auriga* undertook a series of ethically dubious cloning experiments with the Xenomorph species. DNA samples from immediately prior to Ellen Ripley's death were obtained and utilized, with a view to reconstituting and extracting the Queen embryo she had been gestating prior to her suicide. And human kidnap victims were procured with the help of the pirate ship *Betty*, for the purposes of alien impregnation.

A side effect of these experiments was the creation of Clone 8, the first successful clone of Ellen Ripley. Several previous attempts had proved unusable, but Clone 8 survived despite the blending of her DNA with that of the Xenomorph, giving her unusual strength and reflexes, acidic blood, and a telepathic connection to the aliens.

The *Auriga*'s scientists, meanwhile, were able to incubate the Queen itself along with a number of Drones from her eggs. But the creatures managed to escape their confinement, the scientists having underestimated the Xenomorph's natural intelligence and cunning. Evacuation of the human crew was only partially achieved as the aliens proceeded to harvest victims for incubation. As per protocol, the *Auriga*'s emergency systems

automatically plotted a course back to Earth, creating the real possibility of an alien outbreak at home. The remaining crews of the *Auriga* and the *Betty* made the joint decision to crash the *Auriga* into Earth, killing everything on board and with the surviving humans escaping in the *Betty*. Thanks to the *Betty*'s synthetic Call being able to network with the *Auriga*'s systems, this was apparently achieved.

Prior to the crash, Clone 8 encountered the creature known as the "Newborn": a human-Xenomorph hybrid by-product of the Queen's own DNA being accidentally spliced with Ripley's. Clone 8 used her own acidic blood to melt a hole in a window, and the Newborn was terminated by the resultant decompression.

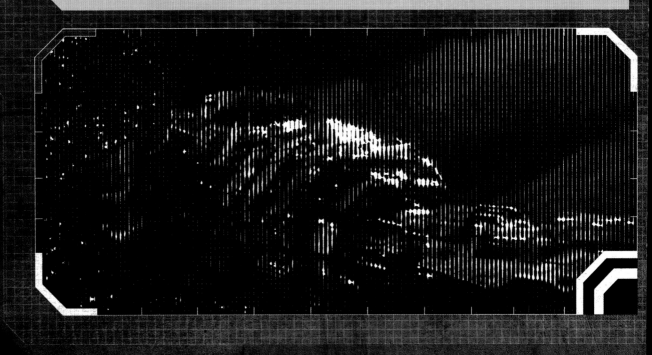

LEFT: USM *AURIGA*, A RESEARCH SHIP, DESCRIBED BY CREW AS "NEW, SHINY, POLISHED, AND MAINTAINED TO PERFECTION." REGISTRATION NUMBER USMRV118.

BELOW: XENOMORPHS HAVE LOW CENTERS OF GRAVITY AND CAN FIT UNDER BAY DOORS BEFORE THEY HAVE OPENED, SO REMAIN LOCKED AND LOADED AT ALL TIMES WHEN ON MISSION.

TOP: THE *AURIGA'S* EXTRA-THICK HULL PLATING ALLOWED STEALTH RUN CAPABILITY.

KEY PERSONNEL

CLONE 8

Clone of Ellen Ripley infused with Xenomorph DNA.

GENERAL MARTIN PEREZ

Captain of the USM *Auriga*, whose role in the cloning experiments was managerial but "hands off." Favored terminating the Ripley clone following extraction of the Queen embryo, but allowed his scientists to overrule him.

DR. MASON WREN

Head of *Auriga*'s scientific staff. Intent on exploiting the Xenomorph for both military and commercial purposes.

DR. JONATHAN GEDIMAN

Auriga scientist. Thought to have been killed early in the Xenomorph outbreak, but was revealed to have been cocooned alive in the Queen's nest.

FRANK ELGYN

Captain of the mercenary smuggling ship *Betty*, employed to deliver kidnapped civilians to the *Auriga* for alien impregnation.

GARY CHRISTIE

Executive Officer aboard the *Betty*. Expert in small arms. Known to favor wrist guns mounted on self-designed extending rigs.

CALL

Synthetic engineer aboard the *Betty*. Revealed to be a solo sleeper agent dedicated to the eradication of the Xenomorph species.

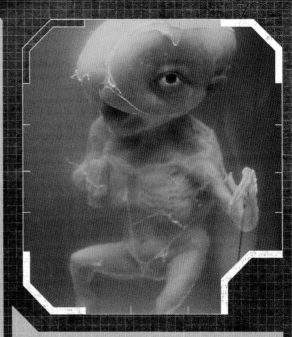

ABOVE: HUMAN/XENOMORPH HYBRID CREATURES IS THE ULTIMATE WEAPON, A GENETIC BOMB THAT WILL TERMINATE BOTH SPECIES, LEAVING ONLY THE NEW CREATURE TO THRIVE. THEY MUST BE STOPPED.

RON JOHNER

Betty crew member. Fearsome in combat and loyal to his crew mates.

DOM VRIESS

Betty crew member. Paralyzed from the waist down due to a previous injury during combat. One of only four survivors of the *Auriga*, along with Clone 8, Call, and Johner.

USM AURIGA / BETTY

The *Auriga* was a United Systems Military research ship, first commissioned in 2369. It was 7,974 feet long, 2,154 feet wide and 1,88 feet high and a maximum velocity of 0.8 light-years per day, as well as a limited stealth run capacity. The latter made it a desirable vessel for clandestine operations, such as the Xenomorph Recreation Project of 2381.

The ship ran on a maximum crew contingent of 49. Its facilities included the usual mess, sleeping, and recreation areas, plus laboratories, containment cells, and a large waste tank. Top of the line during its short life, it was described by one crew member as "new, shiny, polished, and maintained to perfection" under the aegis of General Martin Perez. Its automatic functions were maintained by the "Father" A.I. system: an

evolution of the original MU/TH/ER. It was destroyed in 2381 by the actions of the rogue synthetic Call.

By marked contrast, the *Betty* was small, being about 132 feet by 222 feet by 6 feet. It was a basic twenty-second century transport ship, in a decrepit state by the time of its docking with the *Auriga* in 2381. Multiple decades of ad-hoc repairs with mismatching parts had rendered the ship a patchwork of technologies, but its ultimate functions remained intact. Designed for flight with planetary atmospheres as well as deep space, it had angled side compartments that could be transformed into wings, and a tail fin. Reflecting its piratical later life, its final crew had painted it in camouflage colors to mask its appearance during low-level maneuvers.

PERFECT ORGANISM: QUEEN

Queens are by far the largest form of Xenomorph, often growing to double the size of a standard Warrior and serving as the dominant force in a hive. As egglayers, they are generally rendered immobile by their enormous egg sacs. An egg-laying Queen will also usually be suspended from a high point in a nest, held in place by secreted resin. But they are thought to maintain constant contact with their broods across significant distances by means of telepathy and pheromone secretion.

Queens display most of the distinguishing features of other Xenomorph castes, but they also have unique physical characteristics beyond their size and immobilizing egg sacs. Most immediately obvious is the disproportionately large head carapace, into which the creature's face and mouth can be withdrawn for protection. A similar piece of chitinous armor not found on other castes is present on the Queen's chest, as is a second, possibly vestigial pair of arms.

While vulnerable to some extent when rendered static by the egg-laying phase, Queens are nevertheless extremely difficult to kill. Their extra armor, combined with thickened hides, renders them essentially bulletproof, and their exceptional size and muscle density makes them immensely strong, capable of tearing a human or synthetic in half with their bare hands.

The threat of destruction to their eggs can occasionally halt a Queen's attack—or cause her to call off an attack from her Warriors. But the Queen's most effective defense is more often a vicious offense. Once separated from an egg sac, they are surprisingly agile and display remarkable intelligence. Queens have been witnessed operating machinery. They are also apparently vindictive, and have been seen to pursue enemies tenaciously, even when no longer threatened.

Marine: Do not attempt to engage a Queen at close quarters. Any such action will in almost all cases prove immediately fatal.

QUEEN CREATION

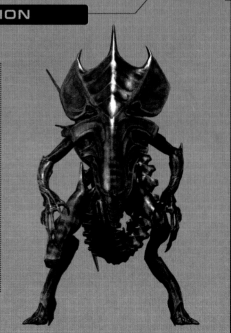

Once again, studies as to the circumstances of a Queen's creation have been inconclusive and sometimes contradictory.

The more generally accepted theory is the introduction of an extra element at the egg stage of development. The synthetic Bishop hypothesized in 2179 that this element could be along the lines of the royal jelly used by bees to create a Queen from a maturing pupa. By this method, a "Royal Egg" would be created, containing a "Royal Facehugger," which would implant a "Royal Chestburster" into its victim. Such a Facehugger is believed to have impregnated Ellen Ripley with a juvenile Queen aboard the *Sulaco*'s escape pod the same year.

More recently, Company scientists have posited that Queens may also be force-evolved from specially chosen Warriors, perhaps once again by the use of a "Royal Jelly" substance. These "hormone storms" are instigated only if an existing Queen is killed or rendered unable to produce eggs.

MARINE BASIC TRAINING:
PLATOON SEPARATION

A U.S.M.C. rifle platoon running at full strength would ideally comprise 25 Marines, 16 of whom make up four rifle teams (with M41 Pulse Rifles) and four gun teams (each with an M56 Smart Gun). A commanding lieutenant leads the platoon, and the rest of the contingent includes drop-ship pilots and copilots, two M577 Personnel Carrier drivers, and two sergeants. Unfortunately, in practice, platoons are often compelled to function with fewer personnel. And in the worst of circumstances, you may find yourself on your own.

Probably the biggest challenge a Colonial Marine will face is the single-unit threat from one or multiple enemies. Of course, prevention is better than cure in this case. The best way to avoid confrontation with a Xenomorph threat alone is not to get separated from your platoon in the first place. But in extreme circumstances where you may find yourself the only—or last—Marine standing, the following tactics—the four Ss—may be the difference between life and death.

① SCAN

Remain hyperaware of your surroundings at all times. Nobody is watching your back, so don't get tunnel vision and keep looking all around, including above. Keep your weapon in the low, ready position, and keep your head and eyes moving.

③ SEARCH

When the threat is more immediate, the search technique is faster than scan. Keep your weapon raised, and your eyes, muzzle, and—where appropriate—target in sync. Fire your weapon only if absolutely necessary. Do not alert additional threats from a wider radius to your location.

② STEALTH

When you have a Xenomorph in your sights, keep it visible and pay close attention to its behavior. If you have not been detected, do nothing to attract its attention. We do not yet understand how the Xenomorph "sees," but it is distinctly possible that sound and movement detection are key elements, so remain silent and keep movements to a minimum. If altering your position is a necessity, do so slowly. Do not rush. Wherever possible, maintain good cover and concealment.

④ SPACE

Keep your distance. Do not get within tail's reach of the Xenomorph, and even more important, never get within reach of its arms or inner jaw. Anecdotal evidence suggests that some castes of Xenomorph are able to spit acid, but in general, long-range attacks are rare. The Xenomorph usually only operates at close quarters. Never forget its speed; you may find yourself at close quarters sooner than you expect.

THIS PAGE: NEVER LET A FATAL INJURY STOP YOU FROM COMPLETING YOUR MISSION. ALWAYS TAKE THAT SHOT. IT MIGHT BE THE LAST ONE YOU TAKE, BUT IF YOU TAKE AN ENEMY WITH YOU, IT WILL BE A GLORIOUS DEATH.

MARINE BASIC TRAINING:
PREPARATION

As an enemy approaches, your squad will probably have less than three seconds to detect the enemy's abilities and plot an attack. *Visualize the enemy in front of you.* What species of Xenomorph is it? What are its strengths? Its weaknesses? Where are you vulnerable? Calculate and memorize your execution strategy. And never forget it. It will save your life. Do it now...

 ASSESS THE THREAT.

 DETECT ENEMY VARIANT.

DEVISE AN ATTACK/DEFENSE STRATEGY.

 PLAN YOUR ATTACK.

 EXECUTE.

135

PERFECT ORGANISM: NEWBORN

Thus far unique in the Company's observations of the Xenomorph species, the so-called "Newborn" was a Xenomorph-human hybrid, and the result of ill-advised cloning experiments aboard the USM *Auriga* in 2381.

A by-product of the process that resulted in the creation of Ripley Clone 8, the Newborn was spawned from a cloned Queen that had become corrupted with human DNA and developed a womb. Taller than a conventional Xenomorph Warrior, it retained the basic skull shape but had rudimentary human facial characteristics, including eye sockets and a nose, as well as a fleshy exterior in place of the Xenomorph's chitinous armor.

Most first-hand accounts agree that the Newborn lacked the Xenomorph's usual tail and inner jaws, although some written reports claim that both features were present. The method of its demise, however—sucked from a small hole in the *Auriga's* hull during a depressurization incident—means that an autopsy was not possible. All specific anatomical details are therefore hearsay.

LEFT AND RIGHT: LACKING ALL THE BIO-MECHANICAL ARMOR OF A XENOMORPH, AND GAINING A BIPEDAL STANCE, FLESHY SKIN, AND NO INNER JAW, NEWBORNS HAVE MANY CHARACTERISTICS OF A HUMAN. IF YOU GET THE CHANCE, THROW THEM OUT INTO SPACE AS SOON AS POSSIBLE.

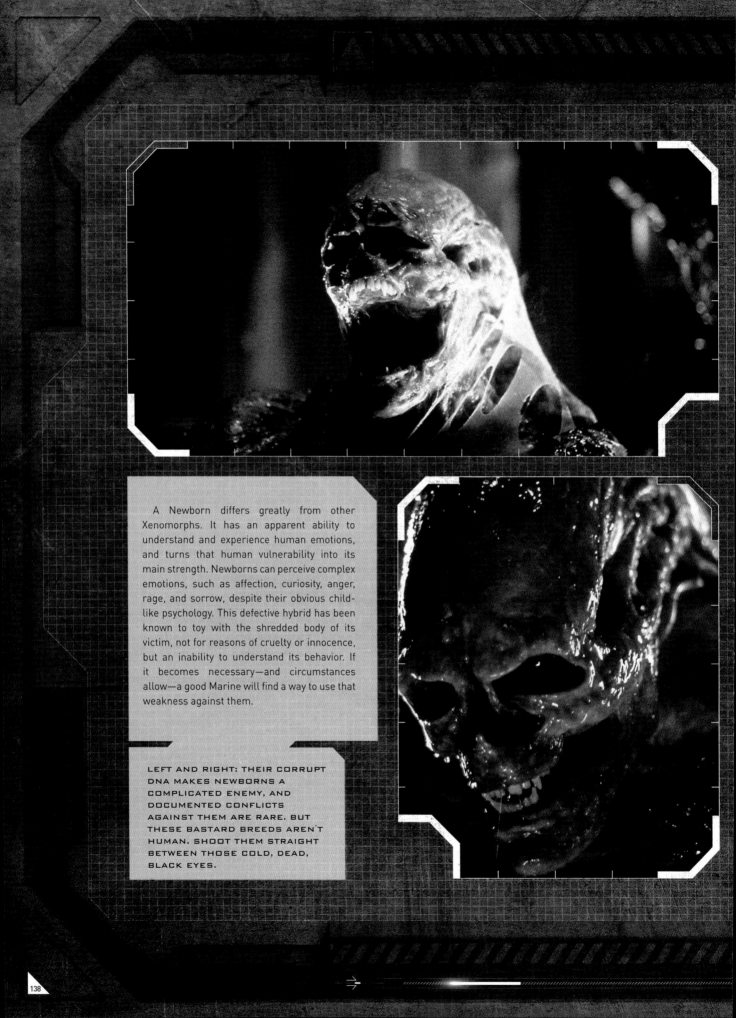

A Newborn differs greatly from other Xenomorphs. It has an apparent ability to understand and experience human emotions, and turns that human vulnerability into its main strength. Newborns can perceive complex emotions, such as affection, curiosity, anger, rage, and sorrow, despite their obvious child-like psychology. This defective hybrid has been known to toy with the shredded body of its victim, not for reasons of cruelty or innocence, but an inability to understand its behavior. If it becomes necessary—and circumstances allow—a good Marine will find a way to use that weakness against them.

LEFT AND RIGHT: THEIR CORRUPT DNA MAKES NEWBORNS A COMPLICATED ENEMY, AND DOCUMENTED CONFLICTS AGAINST THEM ARE RARE. BUT THESE BASTARD BREEDS AREN'T HUMAN. SHOOT THEM STRAIGHT BETWEEN THOSE COLD, DEAD, BLACK EYES.

USM AURIGA TRANSMISSIONS

TRANSMISSIONS FROM THE FIELD CAN PROVIDE VALUABLE INFORMATION ABOUT THE HISTORY AND ORIGINS OF THE ALIEN THREAT, AS WELL AS USEFUL CLUES ABOUT THE WORKINGS OF THE MARINE CORPS. THE FOLLOWING WERE ALL CAPTURED FROM THE USM *AURIGA*, IN ABOUT 2379

" WHO DO I HAVE TO FUCK TO GET OFF THIS BOAT? "
—CLONE 8

" THERE'S A MONSTER IN YOUR CHEST. THESE GUYS HIJACKED YOUR SHIP, AND THEY SOLD YOUR CRYO-TUBE TO THIS... HUMAN. AND HE PUT AN ALIEN INSIDE OF YOU. IT'S A REALLY NASTY ONE. AND IN A FEW HOURS IT'S GONNA BURST THROUGH YOUR RIB CAGE, AND YOU'RE GONNA DIE. ANY QUESTIONS? "
—CLONE 8

" YOU'RE A THING, A CONSTRUCT. THEY GREW YOU IN A FUCKING LAB. "
—CALL, TO CLONE 8

> WEYLAND-YUTANI, RIPLEY'S FORMER EMPLOYER. TERRAN
> GROWTH CONGLOMERATE. THEY HAD DEFENSE CONTRACTS
> WITH THE MILITARY. OH, THEY WENT UNDER DECADES AGO
> GEDIMAN, WAY BEFORE YOUR TIME. BOUGHT OUT
> BY WALMART. FORTUNES OF WAR.
> —WREN

> AT FIRST, EVERYTHING WAS NORMAL. THE QUEEN LAID
> HER EGGS, BUT THEN SHE STARTED TO CHANGE; SHE
> ADDED A SECOND CYCLE. SO THIS TIME THERE IS NO HOST,
> THERE ARE NO EGGS. THERE IS ONLY HER WOMB AND THE
> CREATURE INSIDE. THAT IS RIPLEY'S GIFT TO HER: A HUMAN
> REPRODUCTIVE SYSTEM! AND NOW SHE IS PERFECT!
> —GEDIMAN

> YOU ARE A BEAUTIFUL, BEAUTIFUL
> BUTTERFLY.
> —GEDIMAN, TO NEWBORN

BASIC TRAINING

ALIEN
IDENTIFICATION

ALIEN IDENTIFICATION:
ALL YOU NEED TO KNOW

To accompany Basic Training, all U.S.C. Marines must memorize the following Alien Identification Guide, a vital field manual of hostile alien species you may encounter on any mission. Treat all these enemies with extreme caution. They will kill you, if you don't kill them. Remember: If any members of your squad are exposed to "black goo," spores, Trilobites, or Facehuggers, DO NOT take them back on board your landing craft. Terminate them immediately.

CHEMICAL AO-2959X.91-15

COLLOQUIALLY KNOWN AS "BLACK GOO" AND IMMEDIATELY RECOGNIZABLE AS SUCH. VISCOUS BLACK LIQUID. OFTEN FOUND IN FLASK-LIKE STEOTITE AMPULES.

TRILOBITE

PALE, TRANSLUCENT GRAY IN COLOR. SQUIDLIKE IN APPEARANCE, THE TRILOBITE HAS FOUR LIMBS IN INFANCY BUT HAS BEEN OBSERVED TO DEVELOP MANY MORE AS IT GROWS.

SPORES

VARIATION OF THE ABOVE, HOUSED IN THE FRUIT OF FUNGUS LIKE PLANTS. SPORES BECOME AIRBORNE ONCE RELEASED. INGESTION RESULTS IN GESTATION OF NEOMORPH.

DEACON

BIPEDAL, BLUE-BLACK, SMOOTH-SKINNED ALIEN, STANDING SLIGHTLY TALLER THAN A HUMAN. SIMILAR TO A XENOMORPH WITH A SECONDARY SET OF JAWS AND AN ELONGATED SKULL, ALTHOUGH THE LATTER TAPERS TO A POINT AT THE BACK.

HAMMERPEDE

SNAKE LIKE, GREENISH WHITE IN COLOR, KNOWN TO GROW UP TO 4 FEET 6 INCHES LONG . COBRA-LIKE CRESTED HEAD WITH A FLUKE-LIKE MOUTH.

BLOODBURSTER

INFANT FORM OF NEOMORPH. SMALL ENOUGH TO GESTATE INSIDE A HUMAN HOST, BUT GROWS RAPIDLY ONCE IT EMERGES. PALE, TRANSLUCENT WHITE. QUADRUPEDAL, NOT UNLIKE A SMALL RUNNER.

NEOMORPH

BIPEDAL ALIEN, STANDING 2M TALL WITH TRANSLUCENT WHITE SKIN. FLUKE-LIKE MOUTH, AND ELONGATED SKULL. LONG, SPIKED TAIL. SOME BUT NOT ALL NEOMORPHS HAVE DORSAL SPIKES.

WORKER/DRONE

BIPEDAL ADULT XENOMORPH, TYPICALLY STANDING WELL OVER 6 FEET 6 INCHES TALL. BLACK IN COLOR, WITH AN ELONGATED, SMOOTH DOMED SKULL, THE TOP HALF OF WHICH IS SOMETIMES TRANSLUCENT WHITE. SECONDARY JAWS. SPIKED TAIL. DORSAL TUBING.

FACEHUGGER

CRAB/SPIDERLIKE CREATURE WITH EIGHT FINGERLIKE DIGITS AND A LONG TAIL, APPROXIMATELY 3 FEET LONG. PINKISH BROWN IN COLOR. EXTREMELY FAST. DELIVERY SYSTEM FOR XENOMORPH EMBRYOS.

RUNNER

ADULT XENOMORPH VARIANT WITH A QUADRUPEDAL INSTEAD OF BIPEDAL STANCE. RED/BROWN IN COLOR. ELONGATED, SMOOTH DOMED SKULL, SECONDARY JAWS, AND SPIKED TAIL AS PER DRONE, BUT WITH A LARGER CHEST AND NO DORSAL TUBING.

CHESTBURSTER

INFANT FORM OF CLASSIC XENOMORPH, LIKENED TO A "PENIS WITH TEETH." GESTATES WITHIN A HOST'S CHEST CAVITY. PINKISH BROWN IN COLOR AND ABOUT 1 1 INCHES LONG, INCLUDING TAIL WITH WHICH IT PROPELS ITSELF, SOME HAVE LIMBS, WHILE OTHERS ARE SMOOTH AND PERFECTLY PHALLIC.

WARRIOR

BIPEDAL ADULT XENOMORPH VARIANT. SIMILAR HEIGHT TO DRONE. BLACK IN COLOR WITH THE STANDARD SPIKED TAIL, DORSAL TUBING, AND SECONDARY INNER JAWS, SKULL IS ELONGATED BUT RIDGED INSTEAD OF DOMED.

OVOMORPH

Stage one in the Xenomorph life cycle. The "Egg" contains a Facehugger. Eggs are laid by a Queen. The outer surface is very durable and if penetrated, leaks the same acidic blood as the more developed Xenomorphs that succeed it.

STATISTICS

STATUS: IMMOBILE, SENTIENT, AND DANGEROUS.

HEIGHT // 2 FEET 6 INCHES
COLOR // BLACK-BROWN, BLACK-GREEN

NOTES // ALSO KNOWN AS "EGG," OFTEN FOUND IN LARGE NESTS

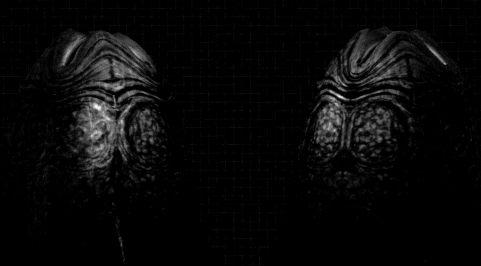

CHESTBURSTER

The Chestburster resembles a large worm and grows in a host, usually following introduction into such by a Facehugger. Following a gestation period, during which the host's DNA may be assimilated with that of the Chestburster, the creature will exit the host in extremely violent fashion.

STATISTICS

STATUS: MOBILE, AGGRESSIVE AND HIGHLY DANGEROUS.

HEIGHT // ONE FOOT OR MORE
WEIGHT // UP TO 20 POUNDS
COLOR // BEIGE

NOTES // RAPID GROWTH RATE; APPEARANCE MAY VARY, DEPENDING ON HOST

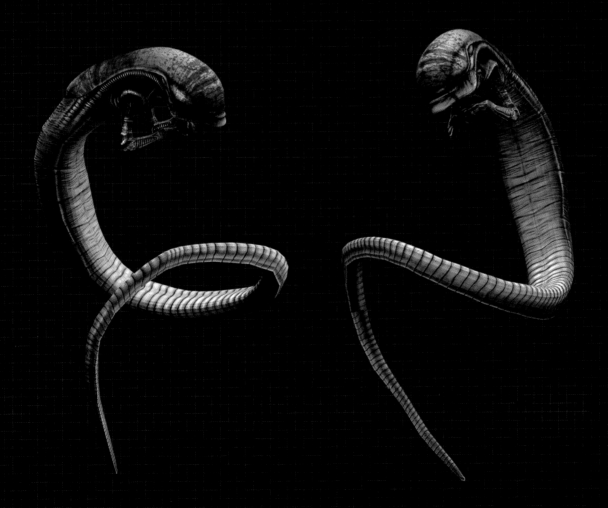

FACEHUGGER

Measuring approximately 3 feet long, the Facehugger is stored in an Ovomorph until a suitable host can be found. The Facehugger implants a Chestburster into said host and then ceases to live.

STATISTICS

STATUS: MOBILE, AGGRESSIVE, AND HIGHLY DANGEROUS.

HEIGHT // 3 FEET
COLOR // BEIGE

NOTES // BONY FINGERLIKE LEGS, SPINELIKE TAIL USED TO ATTACH TO HOST

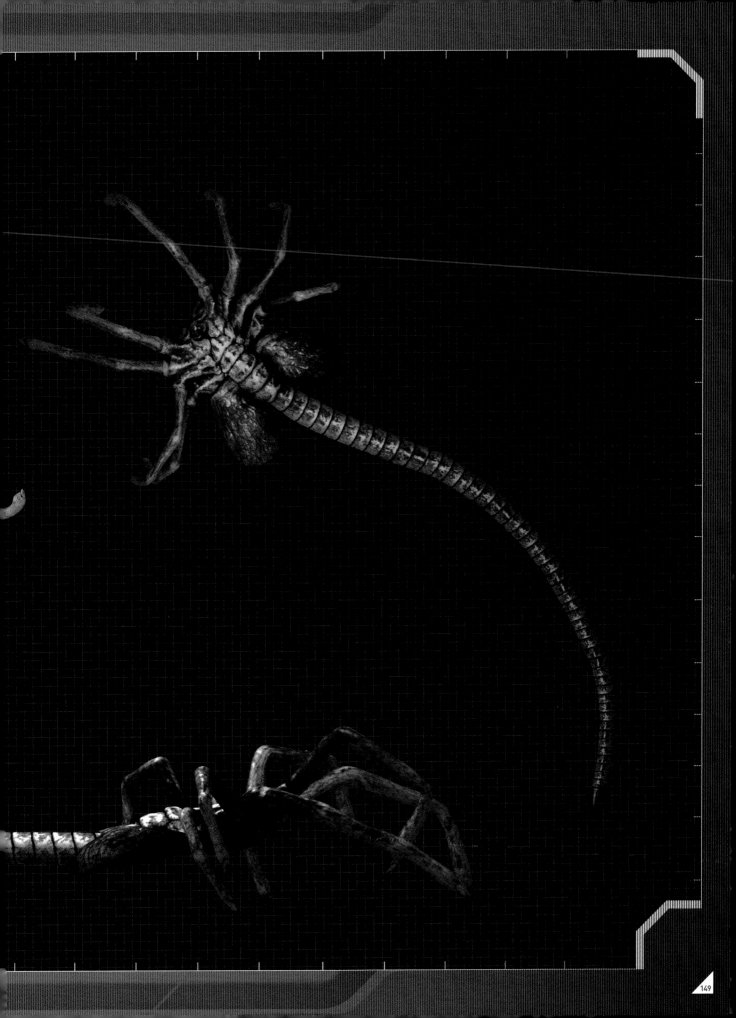

RAVEN

Larger in size than an average Xenomorph, the rarely seen "Raven" is closer to a Queen in size and intelligence. Probably a leader, the Raven walks on two legs and has a ridge of spines on its tail and carapace.

STATISTICS

STATUS: MOBILE, AGGRESSIVE, AND HIGHLY DANGEROUS.

HEIGHT // 10 FEET AND MORE
COLOR // BLACK/GREEN

NOTES // STRONGER AND MORE AGGRESSIVE THAN OTHER XENOMORPHS

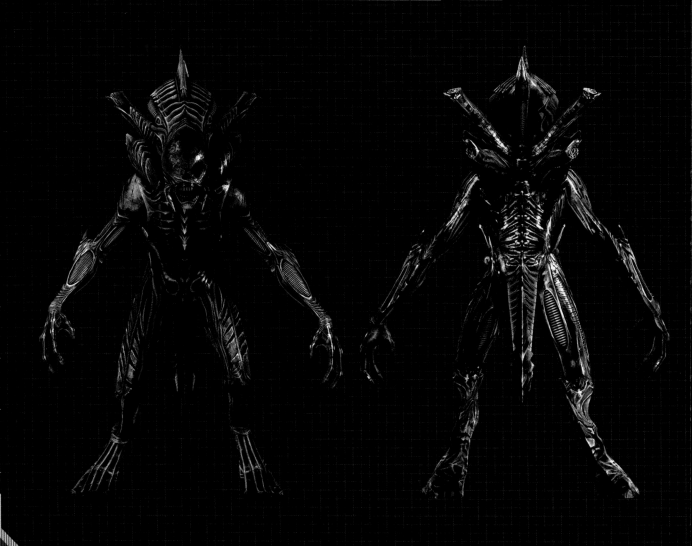

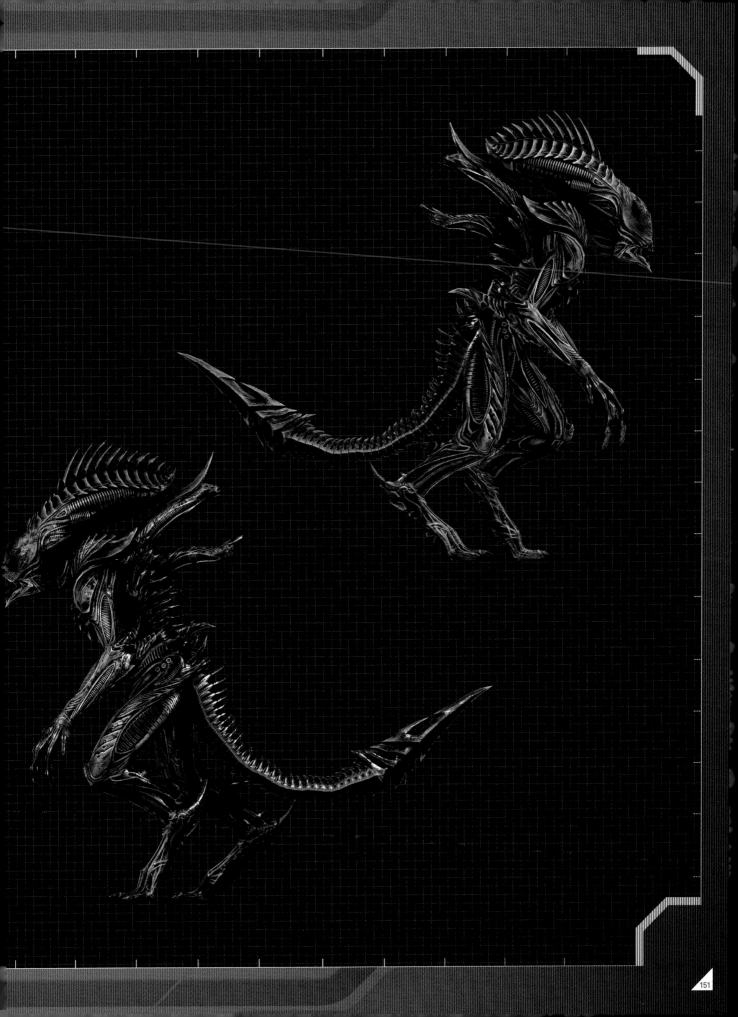

DRONE

One of the most common Xenomorphs, the Drone is thought to be the most basic adult caste of the species. The smooth head carapace is the best identifier for this type. Group and ambush tactics are commonly employed by these creatures.

STATISTICS

STATUS: MOBILE, AGGRESSIVE, AND HIGHLY DANGEROUS.

HEIGHT // 8 FEET
LENGTH // 14 FEET INC. TAIL
SKIN COLOR // BLACK-GRAY

NOTES // SPAWNED FROM HUMAN HOSTS; SMOOTH, DOMED CARAPACE; WILL FOLLOW QUEEN

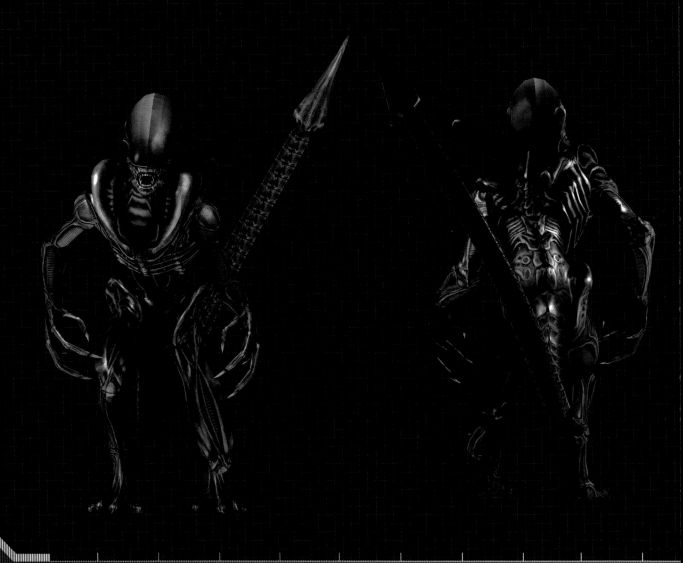

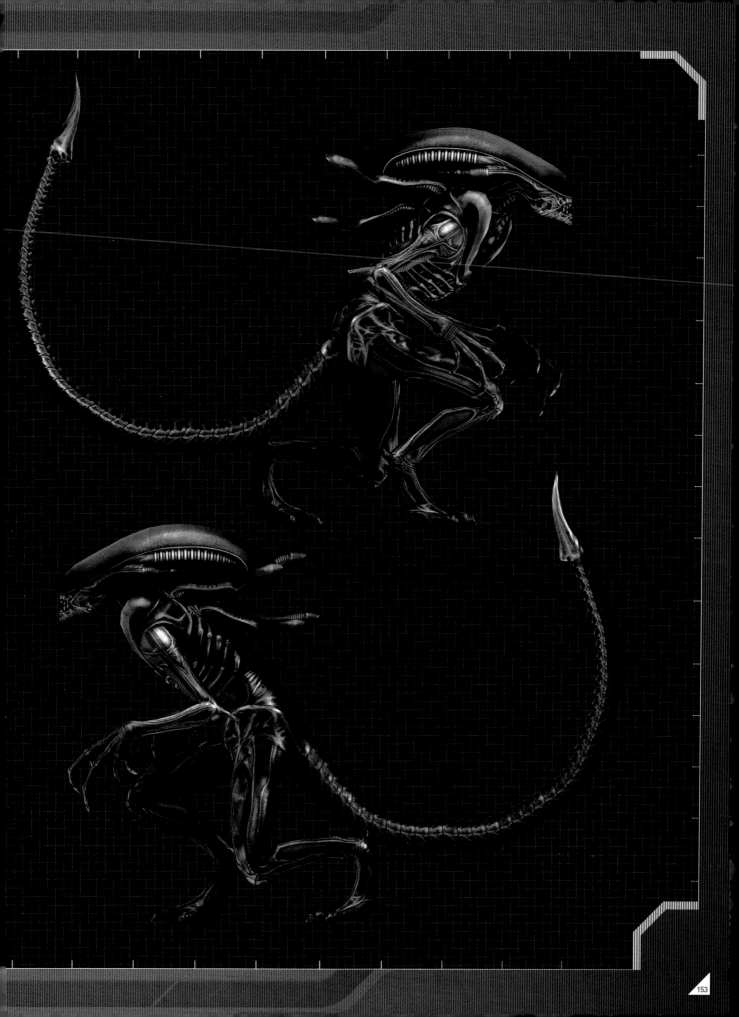

RANGER

This Xenomorph type is best known for spitting acidic blood, which is stored in what seem to be spit gland sacs in the head. It is easily identified by the spines on the head, which flare up to signify that an attack is imminent.

STATISTICS

STATUS: MOBILE, AGGRESSIVE, AND HIGHLY DANGEROUS.

HEIGHT // 8 FEET OR MORE

SKIN COLOR // BLACK-GRAY, BLACK-BLUE

NOTES // LARGE TAIL WEAPON; SPINES ON CARAPACE

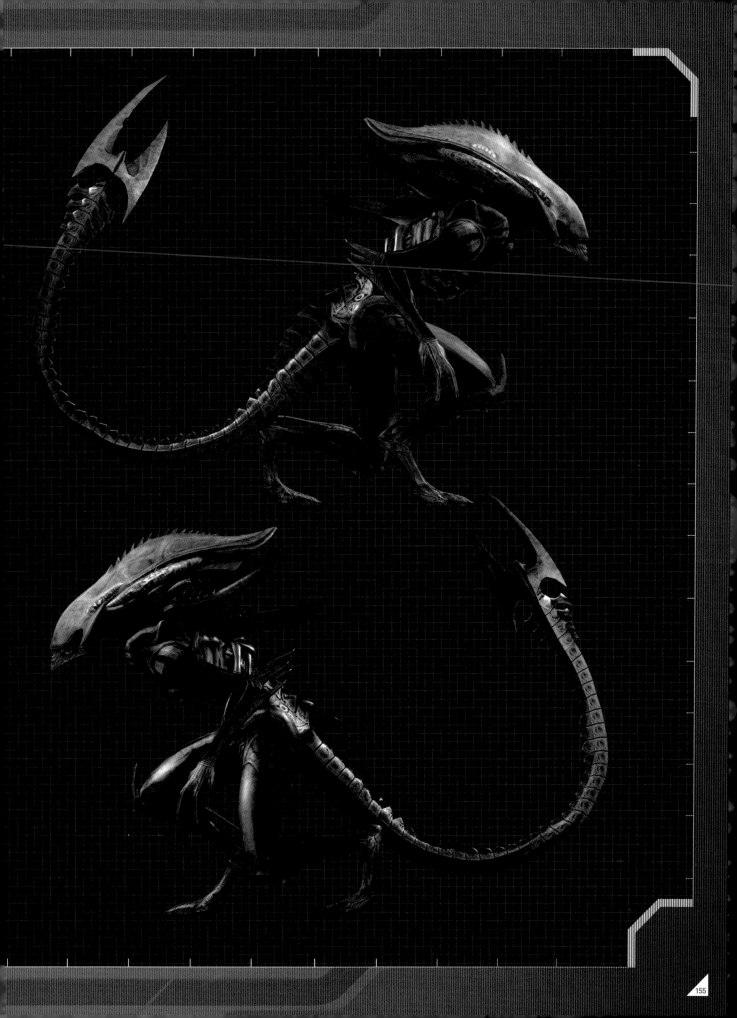

QUEEN

The Queen is usually the biggest and most intelligent Xenomorph. Larger than all other types, the Queen is stronger, too, with an extra set of arms. Queens are highly protective of their eggs, and threatening the latter can be an effective diversion in battle. Queens give birth to all eggs in a hive.

STATISTICS

STATUS: MOBILE, AGGRESSIVE, AND HIGHLY DANGEROUS.

HEIGHT // 15 FEET OR MORE
SKIN COLOR // BLACK, BLACK-BLUE

NOTES // DISTINCTIVE HEAD CREST; EXTRA SET OF ARMS; EGG SACS

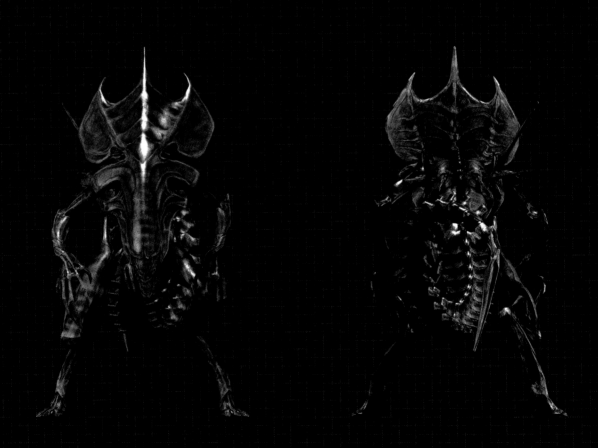

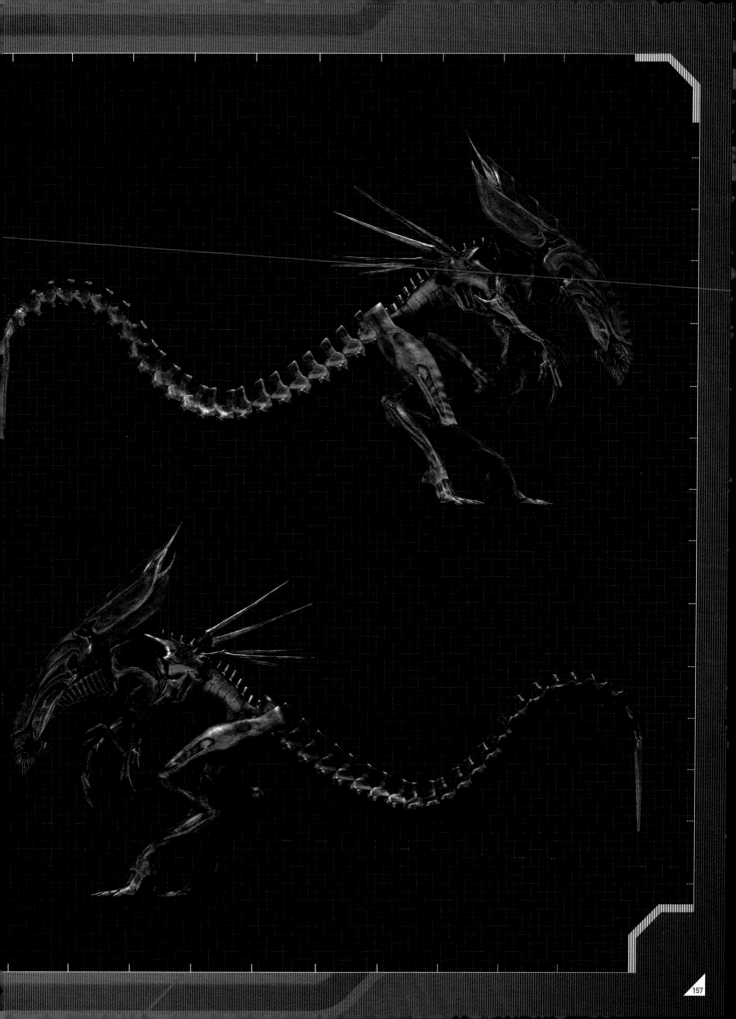

Pre Dissection

Outer Shell   Fetal Inhabitation   Vacant Pod

AN OVOMORPH SKETCH BY THE SYNTHETIC
"DAVID" WHILE ON BOARD USCSS *PROMETHEUS*.

SKETCHED IN 2089 BY "DAVID" WHILE
ON BOARD USCSS *PROMETHEUS.*

U.S.C.M.
THE UNITED STATES COLONIAL MARINE CORPS

" GAME OVER, MAN.
GAME OVER! "
—PRIVATE HUDSON